D0291058

# DRIL

Dril Official "Mr. Ten Years" Anniversary Collection

Printed in the United States of America.

First Edition, 2018

ISBN: 978-1724941688

EMAIL: wint@wint.co

http://wint.co

*This Book Is Dedicated To*
*every One Who Has Ever*
*Died*

# - _PREFACE_ -

*SPECIAL MESSAGE... TO THE FANS, THE SUPPORTERS, "AND YES, EVEN THE TROLLS..."*

to whon it may concern........If you have taken the time and effort to seek out this book, then it is safe to assume that the worst has happened, and that the servers which previously hosted all of my internationally beloved posts have been Permanently Decommissioned by FEMA due to some Jade Helm 15 bull shit, forcing society to scrape together a meager existence within a miserable, Offline Hell.

but fear not bitch, Ive got you covered. me and the boys have slapped together over 400 pages chock-full of these aforementioned posts, after carefully weeding ou t the ones that arent compatible with this particular format, as well as the ones that suck absolute Dick. we're talking Cream of the Crop here, over 1500 perfectly hand-picked portions of Prestige Short Prose.

...and if that weren't enoguh, I personally pulled some strings and managed to recruit the great Leonardo da Vinci, who has generously taken the time out of his busy schedule to get to work adorning over 70 pages of this book with fine Artwork, as a "Bonus." So please say thank you to him.

This book is, without a doubt, the Svalbard Global Seed Vault, of posts, designed to withstand the fall of civilization and ensure that my invaluable Content permeates the hearts and minds of post-collapse generations, in order to prevent the whole of humanity from reverting to the way of the cave man.

Now feel free to kick back, and sit on Ya Ass..... while you enjoy the very best that these Tired Hands have to offer. you've made a wise purchase here. Thank you.

*Thank you.*
*"WINT" @DRIL*

# - *TABLE OF CONTENTS* -

*"animals can have spirit animals too."*

**wint**
**@dril**

in veneration of the right honorable baroness my six komodo dragons will be rewarded one etxra " DIPEY CHANGE " and allowed to eat spaghetti

3212657308836373504

**wint**
**@dril**

koko the talking ape.. has been living high on the hog, wasting our tax dollars on high capacity diapers. No more. i will suplex that beast,

5084708309812183O4

**wint**
**@dril**

i fear my tropical fish no longer respect me after i accidetnally stumbled backwards & smushed my ass hole right up against their $3000 tank

843885268805599232

**wint**
**@dril**

someone please verify rumor that petsmart is turning all animals loose (lizards snakes rats dogs) because of the scoundrel obama care

555779639332044801

**wint**
**@dril**

bring me your dead pet and i will make a sword out of it for $39

497132363911299072

penning a heartwarming screen play about a horse who wins nascar

wint
@dril

9791420649852682226

thinking aobut turning into a wolf and kicking hurricane sandys ass

wint
@dril

883352279558049794

committing unforgivable crimes against nautre in my laboratory ,trying to create the next genetically discombobulated meme animal

wint
@dril

6137889392293355552

having to hose off 900 screaming animals at my job at the zoo every day is harder than any thing a untied states marine ever did

wint
@dril

986438992529936384

the pursuit of having trhe nicest opinions online... is the only thing that separates us from the god damn animals. the sole reason we exist

wint
@dril

699436292057272320

**wint** @dril

need someone in or around geigertown, philadelphia to help me dispose of approx 7500 live guinea pigs. i can not pay you, i will not pay you

32882019272753152

 **wint** @dril

BOSS TELLS ME I CAN KISS MY FERRETS AT WORK, BUT NO OPEN MOUTH. I PUNCH THE FLOOR SO HARD HIS SCREEN SAVER DEACTIVATES

256431328592011266

 **wint** @dril

i am selling six beautfiul, extremely ill, white horses. they no longer recognize me as their father, and are the Burden of my life

504134967946141697

 **wint** @dril

what is quickest way to get sprayed by a skunk in a discreet maner

331623917913505793

 **wint** @dril

ill be hiding under the floorboards and snorting herbs for stress relief energy until i am ready to face my guinea pigs again

214982778658369537

i did eat an ant farm once

wint
@dril

476963823858249728

my dog approaches me, rolls over on its back, and i vomit all over its stomach. undoing 9 years of trust with this animal

wint
@dril

993932033813614592

dear horseshoe crab,: you are neither of those things, and yyou look like a damn rat in a hat

wint
@dril

545473896087289856

*"the essential, Male Ass"*

YoshiGod9 says that if you shit into a wasp nest they wont sting your ass because theyre too dumb to know what shit even is. Prove him wrong

wint
@dril

164752101191335936

known among variety of local retailers as "oily ass man." banned from mattress giant, pier 1 imports, ikea, raymour & flanigan, and so forth

wint
@dril

195746945095045121

calling it: SimAss from Maxis will be 1991's hottest title. greatest Ass simulator I have ever had the pleasure of using.

wint
@dril

218845364806103041

do not strain the ass. the best way to take a shit is to electrocute yourself and let it all shoot out naturally. never strain the ass.

wint
@dril

217428546430316547

i will never apologize for my ass no matter how many people close their accounts. i will never apologize for the gestures i make with my ass

wint
@dril

311293641782079488

my ass looks like a Stooge's ass

wint
@dril

808173934004891648

listen., pal, if you think im the kind of guy who doesnt wipe his ass, you're barkin up the wrong tree. my ass needs all the help it can get

wint
@dril

593884480332558336

my ass has become too powerful for even me to contorl. tonight , i will sit on the hibachi grill at benihana and put an end to this hell

wint
@dril

222829471194030081

as a teen the docotr told me my ass cheeks would grow into a normal mans size instead of looking like fucked up hockey pucks. another lie

wint
@dril

245308603785949184

invented by god in Year 666, my sickening Ass was tasked with torturing insubordinate angels until it fell into the hands of the shit prince

wint
@dril

184004539723153408

please don't use asterisks to censor words, they look like tiny assholes and make everything worse

wint
@dril

26878008485

pulls down pants revealing ass. pulls down pants further, revealing a 2nd pair of ass cheeks. pulls them down still fruther, revealing 3rd p

wint
@dril

1776150602382213 12

sometimes i wish my ass would be destroyed by a meteor just so i wouldn't have to take shits anymore

wint
@dril

221786712962113536

i stumble into a nameless town and see an ass pressed up against a screen door. i instinctively turn around and walk back towards the desert

wint
@dril

324771122941923328

to the fine folks who kicked my bare ass while i was trapped in the automatic door at walmart: why do you people insist on punishing success

wint
@dril

3965862616 13252608

my ass looks like a fucking frankensteins ass

wint
@dril

882812931355889664

my massive shoulder span constantly prevents my tiny ,malnourished ass from absorbing sunlight. my body is essentially at war with its self

wint
@dril

448087941802622976

got a big piece of velcro stuck to my big ass

wint
@dril

845863995781402624

my opionon on people who use the word "ass" is as follows: these people dont exist to me, therefore ih ave no opinion of them. theyre rotten

wint
@dril

216620032069873664

ass is the most poisonous part of the human

wint
@dril

466860932736368642

"im sorry for claiming i was going to "flip the script" on dry rub barbeque. that was wildly irresponsible of me"

**wint**
@dril

i'll be wrapping this hog in tinfoil to protect my dryrub from the NSA until all this bluster dies down

366320370057363456

**wint**
@dril

i cannot eat this bowl of rice until i've personally applied a louisiana-style dry rub to each grain. i refuse to eat like a peasant

347066858081509376

**wint**
@dril

so the wisdom i gained in exile with the barbecue shaman on the peak of Mt. DryRub is apparently non-transferable to Yale. sad and upset

145760583885660160

**wint**
@dril

famous daves proud to announce confessional booths in every restaurant where you can go to atone for your bbq sins. fucking murder me

134480227324805122

**wint**
@dril

i refuse to patronize Famous Dave's BBQ until they throw cultural sensitivities to the wind and change their name back to "the piss morgue"

181583390959603713

wint
@dril

finest rack o ribs youve ever seen. you get your favorite dry rub all over that badboy but- oh no- it's sand. the sand laughs #BBQNightmares

167687684607848448

wint
@dril

reading a 900 page book on Dry Rubs and immediately forgetting all of it and just dumping a shit load of cocoa pebbles on my ribs

835956134179663873

wint
@dril

"the key to making that steak sizzle is to get a nice dry rub from your dry rub man, and prayer. prayer fucking owns" - sun tzu or some shit

233011295220297728

wint
@dril

im going to eat this entire rack of baby back ribs in protest of nasa's bullshit robot on mars

217436119124549632

*"mind of a lion.. heart of a Pregnant woman"*

I Love say ing shit like, "At the Louvre, Even the BATHROOMS are nice"

wint
@dril

898207281631854593

ironing my suspender straps and treating them with powders... in the privacy of my study...making the nit wits and losers absoltuley furious

wint
@dril

793928275898818560

male model: washing my luxurious long hair is so boring. i wish my entire body was bald like you
me: Now the healing can begin

wint
@dril

523825326506647552

im getting my rat tail chrome plated in 2015

wint
@dril

511836385385656320

strongest blade in the world, howeve,r it is so fragile as to shatter when handled by any force other than the delicate touch of a lesbian .

wint
@dril

235218148800991233

do not be afraid to talk to that lonely boy on the train ... with the rosy red cheeks, sun glasses & big cigar... he just mmight be... angel

wint
@dril

551464123293523968

hauling ass to the hair place to find tekken chauncey and laying into him with a rolled up newspaper while hes getting a Perm

wint
@dril

1008048712902463488

attn: fucked up t-shirts incorporated-- get me a tweety bird with devil horns saying "I refuse to pay for a car wash"

wint
@dril

502846777218072576

seeing the hospital workers dreessed in pajamas?? like "seriously?" im a sleepys mattress professional. id get killed for wearing that trash

wint
@dril

496332146320355328

yeah thats right babe... im in the shower right niow.. wearing nothin but a neon green tracksuit, and some belts

wint
@dril

498555384890941441

going to be doing some extremely powerful introspective poses on the railroad track for the next couple hours, so please cancel all trains

**wint**
**@dril**

498517110185005057

i vow to continue improving my Posture uuntil my chest consumes the earth

**wint**
**@dril**

516549414794825728

all young men Must be fitted for a good Italian suit, ideally by age 4. i will not fucking apologize or back down from this

**wint**
**@dril**

577456969734316032

im at the point in my life where i cant relate to any popular fictional characters unless they use massive amounts of hair gel and steriods

**wint**
**@dril**

579772207217422336

shame on you for assuming I tattooed "Yes Yes Ya'll" on my newborn infant's head for a less than 100% justifiable reason

**wint**
**@dril**

138816408611074049

big meeting with chinese investors coming up in 5 minutes. need to look sharp and presentable. im running my dick under the faucet

wint
@dril

655511275070443520

having my Balls exfoliated by a Doctor

wint
@dril

859141345453191169

i know i will catch endless flak for this. but I am of the belief, that the tried and true Suit and Tie, is a Classic

wint
@dril

645275464664240128

i get dozens of compliments about my perfect ears every day. it's llike Shut the fuck up. Im trying to eat a bagel in my car and you do this

wint
@dril

478895776395841538

((attempts to dress up for hte first time in my life to attend Grandmas funeral but ends up looking like a school shooter from the matrix)

wint
@dril

824570907838517248

#WorldwideHandsomeDay looking dumb as a dog in my piss-yellow tuxedo whilst i spend hundres of dollars on international phone calls

wint
@dril

937344504872558593

daily reminder that i wear a suit and tie daily eeven though I have not set foot in public for over 16 years #GoodBoy #Hansdome

wint
@dril

462230308457181185

i love wearing clothes with words on them. like a fucking caveman

wint
@dril

375833092755169280

man encased in lethal amounts of body oil and skin bronzer preserved for thousands of year.s.. beautiful

wint
@dril

567745273557164032

"*its the weekend baby. youknow what that means. its time to drink precisely one beer and call 911*"

sorry bartender. if i order the wrong beer the trolls will have a field day. lets play it safe. fiji water for me, with a Hint of pepsi

wint
@dril

578619277651132418

top me off, beer man. here's to bottoms up **gets kicked out of the fucking establishment for putting my dirty coat on the bar*

wint
@dril

555138278400483328

drunk driving may kill a lot of people, but it also helps a lot of people get to work on time, so, it;s impossible to say if its bad or not,

wint
@dril

464802196060917762

please tell me I wasnt the only one screaming at the tv last night, begging for one of the VP candidates to recognize budweiser's sacrifices

wint
@dril

256755112863756289

the Original bad boys!! the Best, the very greatest. That's right folks, ive got the Whazzup Budweiser Men on board to film 17 short films

wint
@dril

22043730972

wint
@dril

Im about to get wild at 2:30am on this Fucking can of #Beer I found. I am going to use my grandpas knfie to "Shot Gun" it. #ThingsILikeToDo

282389722779746305

wint
@dril

i need towels sent to my house . this is not a fucking joke this time

282392709350686720

wint
@dril

ME: there is a new type of beer called "Wine" shirtless guy witht 104 followers: Shut the fuck up
ME: Yes sir

779812111249772544

wint
@dril

our list of demnads: 1) sportscenter on adult swim. non-negotiable 2) votig booths with beer in them 3) plastic bags to kill ourselves with

248262294478397440

wint
@dril

steel reserve 211 extra high gravity breast milk

1027714982652207104

**wint**
@dril

cant wait to dip a paint roller in my preferred brand of beer and suck it like a big yeti dick

502346449225809920

**wint**
@dril

Why am i smilin tonight fellas? Just got my hands on that new good treat to sip known only as simply "Bber".

577286362396676096

**wint**
@dril

im going to watch homer simpson sing the beer song on you tube. does anyone care to join me

14250305134

**wint**
@dril

drinking beer out of a humming bird feeder because all of my glasses have bug's in them

992112258380640257

"*live free or die. kfc*"

most famous birds: 1.Krfc 2. talking parrot who said "i love you" the night he died 3. thanksgiving turkey 4. tweety bird 4(Tie). Phoenix

wint
@dril

475493686172987393

i bought one of those craigslist peacocks. this fucking thing wont eat and its loud

wint
@dril

391834671329193984

i tried to throw a molotov cocktail at a bird but he was too high up

wint
@dril

393166104438124544

these shitty birdseed husks my canary rejected will make a fine Car

wint
@dril

26513897027

my friend the only crypto currency you wanna get your hands on is this: bird seed. There is a lot of birds and they all gotta eat

wint
@dril

945649210455707648

sometimes i gaze towards the beautiful endless sky and wish that i was a bird. so that i could piss and shit out of the same hole

wint
@dril

350803350817751040

kfc sextuple down is back. pieces of lettuce and tomato encased in perfect cube of processed bird. "The most vile fucking thing imaginable"

wint
@dril

481864984427634688

kfc commercial idea: a man is trying to get into kfc but he is too small to reach the door handle. he tries and tries and nobody helps him

wint
@dril

595394392023760896

rubbinb hand sanitizer all over my loud mouthed pet birds

wint
@dril

525653873688870914

relaly hoping this election isnt a repeat of '04, when i got trapped in a brushpile and mistakenly voted for a bird

wint
@dril

265675646775205889

getting pecked by birds like a dick head

wint
@dril

997018507228278784

every year, a figure dressed in black leaves three crispy strips & a bottle of mtn dew at the kfc man's grave then disappears into the night

wint
@dril

149380193922977792

a mother bird tends to her young until my big sweatpants ass slowly pushes her nest off of the tree

wint
@dril

207347124457844736

kick birdseed into my neck as i tumble down a muddy staircas e into a pile of fluorescent lightbulsb while 100 tiny shits rolldown my pant

wint
@dril

25522593060

my birth name is "KFC Sunflower", but you can call me "Shit"

wint
@dril

230463002455982080

**wint**
**@dril**

the entire contents of the kfc smokehouse angus chicken snacker slide out and fall directly into my shirt. "IM FUCKED" i yell out

776324289893175296

**wint**
**@dril**

im inventing a new kind of bird seed out of sand and waste

15791972842

**wint**
**@dril**

PigPissClyde hid in a bush for 2 hrs and took secret photos of PigPissLou wiping bird shit off his windshield with a chipotle bag. Pure win,

356180315594702848

"*nothing more heartwrenching than having to look a man in the eye and say "pal, your brand is nonsense. not even the gurus can salvage this.*"

**wint**
**@dril**

Perhaps the tier I aspire to achieve the most is that of the Milk Bone brand. Such flawless precisIon. Beauty; Grace. Truly awe inspiring .

362217634374238208

**wint**
**@dril**

ME: why am i just the man for the job? lets see. i love hamburgers, i love to help, HAMBURGER HELPER CEO: Leave these hallowed halls at once

598672627515916288

**wint**
**@dril**

i've been blacklisted from hollywood simply because I refuse to compromise my unwavering support of Microsoft brand and product. cowardice

422743071193710593

**wint**
**@dril**

(pitching the Michelin Man) hes this big white dipshit and people associate him with tires for some reason. he has no personality. no jokes

630824369581891584

**wint**
**@dril**

Q: Would you describe your Brand as more "Uday" or "Qusay" hussein?
A: Qusay, without a doubt. Qusay.

767732814141853696

pleased to announce that i will shatter all barriers in 2017 by becoming the first adult gerber baby

wint
@dril

827370147920879616

my agent says if i get my balls neutered off ill be able to calm down & improve my posts. but i keep telling him, my posts wil never be good

wint
@dril

754126927854796800

Yeah, some of us like to network with successful brands on twitter. The rest of you want to join hippy communes and suck the hippys' dicks.

wint
@dril

350289248907296770

been thinking about it a lot, and i do not believe that anyone will ever come up with a brand name better than "Taster's Choice"

wint
@dril

959224429636214786

Sponsor Wanted: Basically U Would Pay Me to eat Dogfood and i go "Its So Good Even Humans Can Eat It" or just fucking ignore me until i die

wint
@dril

317752683996057600

*circles "become gay" on a whiteboard*

wint
@dril

351333534734106625

i do print my posts out on index cards and dead drop them at city hall. you have to get your teeth in the game, other wise youre just shit

wint
@dril

383735617495920640

thinking i only have about 80000 more posts to read before i figure out the precise amount of sex that should be allowed in pepsi commercals

wint
@dril

1000284468932902917

i will nbe referring to a certain soda brand as "p*psi" until i receive the $16 they owe me for years of aggressive social content strategy

wint
@dril

326854857682190340

the ceo of cash4gold just called me, crying. he tells me this—he says people arent respecting his brand on twitter. i fucking hate this site

wint
@dril

387766389353639936

one thing my brand will never associate itself with is piles of filthy leaves

wint
@dril

363348650631512064

head fully immersed in kfc bucket filled with hidden valley ranch dressing and m&ms. brand engagement locked in at one hundred percent

wint
@dril

505108758641795072

ideally...Sleepys Mattress Professionals will get on board with printing "DRIL TWEETS" on-product, and pull both our brands out of the Abyss

wint
@dril

923393294964535298

atticus quiznos, cornelius pepboys, baron von sega; distinguished luminaries who voluntarily castrated themselves for the sake of the #Brand

wint
@dril

397126702821670912

after careful consideration, ive decided to fuck the green m&m because they made it look like a girl. i would not fuck the red or yellow m&m

wint
@dril

399334112357384192

wint
@dril

i see jokes like "doge". like "angry cat". and I think to myself, "This is fucking actually good. How can I interface this with my strats."

403894334627409921

wint
@dril

i got a booth set up outside of the casper, WY red lobster to promote & expand my brand presence. if you speak to me i will call the police.

340239339726462977

wint
@dril

cant deal with people who have such an utter disregard for brand integrity that they would log on without a shirt. this is not a pornno.

324545306408677376

wint
@dril

i believe in sex. i work with asphalt and i respect the asphalt. pain is my god and heaven. i am NOT a GAMER DU CASUAL. sponsored by nestle

326854857682190340

wint
@dril

nobody at PepsiCo, the parent company of Pepsi & Frito-Lay, uses bathrooms. this comapny prides itself on hiring people who never shit.

434846987725180928

**wint**
@dril

everyrtfhing I say and do is owned hereforth by the fine individuals of the Cash For Moms Online corporation. i beLieve in cash for moms. ..

389758990717956096

**wint**
@dril

i changed my mind. fuck cash for moms online. fuck it all. its nonsense that moms are given allthis good cash while I make $0.003 per tweet

389764663002423296

**wint**
@dril

Just got chemical castrated in exchangge for a free oil change at pep boys #Dealmaker #Boss

962226290257428480

**wint**
@dril

the emerald nuts corporation deducts my pay substantially for each death thrreat i receive so please stop it

479105655811629056

**wint**
@dril

diseased hogs pissimg everywhere but the toilet. wads of hair covered in piss and smashed into the floor #SponsoredContent

540156335527329792

the new meat ball sub's sandwich at mc donalds is a home run and between you and me the taste is sensational and almost good

wint
@dril

586175582066577408

"before we begin todays ball game, user @dril would like a few words on Dairy Queen" the audience boos as i traipse the field in my tiny car

wint
@dril

612298274733707264

just deleted 23,000 tweets at the request of Sbarro. feeling Purified

wint
@dril

617798718461358081

for the 9th time today a complete stranger has approached me on the street and told me to go suck some ass. "And still the brand endures"

wint
@dril

982827352026697728

sort of bullshit that im not allowed to be the wendy's mascot just because im repugnant to most people & woudl negatively impact their sales

wint
@dril

346647087527624704

my lawyer has just informed me that my official logo resembles an alien with a big dick. this is the My Lai Massacre of personal branding

wint @dril

256024133811453952

people have been printing lots of swears on hot sauce labels as of late

wint @dril

274436470830399488

to the fanboy who threw acid iat my face near fuddrucker`s, you can destroy my body but The Cloud will preserve my brand for millennia #PS4

wint @dril

304502088757563392

i feel truly blessed ,knowing that everyone who has spoken ill of my brand is eating bugs in a cold prison cell.

wint @dril

664808380226281472

"*The reason the "Cars" movies have gained so much popularity is becuase the cars speak to one another. You don't get that with real life cars*"

my favorite part of nascar is when I vomit all over my shirt and car after the race., desecrating the logos of the brands that enslave me

wint
@dril

481075773583794176

turning my headlights off when driving at night,.. so that my Rivals cannot see me

wint
@dril

681607955498799105

look out for the car with the words "INCEST DEATH" painted on the hood thats always going like 20-30 mph under the speed limit, that ones me

wint
@dril

207344876239597568

I Just cried for 9 hrs because i realized i will never have my own Faerie, and NOw i gotta get my car inspected?? SEriously? Are U for REAL

wint
@dril

224772799955353600

running multiple red lights while listening to the radio jockeys Flawless "dr. evil" impersonation and scream-laughing

wint
@dril

862054746806296576

i dont think the monster truck gravedigger has ever dug any actual graves. it would be a very disrespectful and loud way to do it

wint
@dril

436644736079003649

truthfully, i do believe that, now thatm the gas prices are low, i think that theres going to be a lot less BULL S#!T on the commute !!

wint
@dril

555653412038397952

my idea for a car, is that it looks like a normal car., but right next to the steering wheel Blammo. theres a hose you can suck beer out of

wint
@dril

589509663256870912

(fantasizing about dangling off hood of my moving car adn touching the truck nuts on the jeep in front of me with tongue) hell yea, actually

wint
@dril

476758780013576192

i love spending 10000 dollars to make my car loud as shit and suck ass

wint
@dril

868171031978049536

wint
@dril

cruising the streets of night time in my Hyundai Sonata... looking for drunk drivers to ram into

923760126305153024

wint
@dril

kelly bluebook is my gf

768572081042780160

wint
@dril

ok. so apparently throwing knives at my car is A Thing now. apparently my Emphatic Capitalization is frowned upon by People Who Read Words

377940715600240641

wint
@dril

please banky. if youre out there reading this i need you to graffiti a chode with balls on my shop teacher's station wagon

13408460615983104

wint
@dril

posing next to a jeep and handing out business cards at the high school i graduated from 8 years ago, explicitly stating i do NOT followback

353376007077625857

GM developing car seats which detect how wet your ass is and post the data onto your facebook page, for fun?? fuck eveory thing about this .

wint
@dril

243024182856798210

i can infer that the owner of this car with "Wade" painted on the hood is either named "Wade" or enjoys the word "wade" for personal reasons

wint
@dril

4070597013066642432

more bullshit: enterprise rent-a-car will refuse to serve you if you imply that youre wearing a cock ring, even if its for health reasons

wint
@dril

237928124183105536

as sure as i am a VETERAN`S SON , i will never move over and let an emergency vehicle pass me , no matter how loud it is

wint
@dril

902825560015032320

picture now, on this Warm Summer's Night, if all the "SWEARS" on this page were replaced with helpful links to mazda "Sign and Drive" events

wint
@dril

893005663022067712

**wint**
@dril

the road is a battle field, all the other cars are your enemies, and not using turn signals gives you an Advantage against then

1027088072066789377

**wint**
@dril

i had that dream abgain... the one where im at the coliseum, annihilating shitloads of roman gladiators by drifting around in my macktruck

815279829746667520

**wint**
@dril

if trucks can wear nuts Then i should be allowed to nail yosemite sam mudflaps to my asscheeks

218515764930547715

**wint**
@dril

never too old to imprint "SABRINA THE TEEN AGE WITCH" itnto the hood of your car multiple times with big metal boots #SellOuts #FakePeople

115447181246337024

**wint**
@dril

if you go to a nascar rally carrying a clipboard and wearing a hard hat people will just let you go on the track and kiss all the good cars

569848814758170624

Make normal car horns "LOUDER"
Make Fire Engines, Ambulances and Police
Cars "LESS LOUD"

wint
@dril

908883949262442496

just planted my big ass through a mans wind
shield while trying to get my shirt out of a
tree

wint
@dril

915031069774241792

*"you all can send me breast milk now. thank you"*

**wint**
@dril

if each of my followers send me 1 rag i might be able to clean up all the messes in my house

399618911609442304

**wint**
@dril

if youre a healthy young male or female with blood type O, please consider donating a kidney to me. my goal is 22 kidney 's

396292163828318210

**wint**
@dril

once againl, the "legalize incest" crew has somehow hijacked the protest I organized to ban sorcerers from congress

256027929845321728

**wint**
@dril

to my mates online: im raising $1900 so i can drink a ton of olive oil to see if it turns to shit when i shit it out or just stays olive oil

517849949737070592

**wint**
@dril

patreon up by $4000/month since i got removed from out back steakhouse for calling all the waiters homos and became a Freedom of Speech guru

982703760802795520

cumstarter. i need 500 liters of cum to start a projec.t i dont know its some bacon blog. who gives a fuck

wint
@dril

1975061761817313330

sorry. my "wrestle a pile of huge dildos for charity" event was a total imbroglio. all proceeds raised must now go towards my hospital bill

wint
@dril

3053459471210946566

KICKSTARTER: buy me a big roll of bubble wrap so i can fuck it --- $0.23 Pledged of $35 Goal -- -

wint
@dril

1754723921209753600

unfortunately the red cross does not accept blood that you foundi n the trash can or blood that has been coughed up into your shitty beard

wint
@dril

1775695845288919040

i'm pepsi rep kevin and we need $12m kickstarter dollars to make a pepsi commercial in true 8 Bit. lets show this new pope what were made of

wint
@dril

3120900646897213440

if youre sick of Incest, please support Anti Incest by changing your avatar red. if your avatar already has green tint then please remove it

2347194140

consider this: the time and energy it took for you to tell me to "Shut the fuck up" could have instead been used to breast feed 10 orphans .

925749254374723584

thank you all. your kind donations of $400000 will keep me alive for 1 more month, after being fired for looking at racist swords on my ipad

6246598847184281460

MarioGodKenneth is stuck in israeli prison again and ive received $0 in donations towards his bail.

614933969277222912

what my organization does is take fatsuits from obnoxious PG-13 comedies and donate them to the needy

38426127315767296

*"judges are bullshit, your honor"*

**wint**
@dril

am i correct in assuming that everyone is happy about prisons not being private anymore because now we get to see the inmates dick and asses

766336774784376833

**wint**
@dril

i scan the docs & id the perp. "The Radio Shack Masturbator". bounty on his head. i put 100 bullets into my pistol and hit the god damn road

346643803362443265

**wint**
@dril

The SHeriff's Department Denies Your Request To Be Sat On By Muscle Ladies As Punishment And Would Like For You To Pay Your Ticket With Cash

326384487120375808

**wint**
@dril

scenario: i'm sitting in the dentist's chair getting my cavities filled. a stray pube enters the window and lands in my mouth. who's liable

256795162993377280

**wint**
@dril

every now and then i like to treat myself to a bit of "Lying under oath"

677807566949347329

"Ur honor, if Mr Pibb was truly this man's uncle, then surely hed be able to dazzle us with Pibb Merch"
JUDGE:damn he's right. No Pibb Merch

wint
@dril

459369149387784193

"jail isnt real," i assure myself as i close my eyes and ram the hallmark gift shop with my shitty bronco

wint
@dril

181225396694560769

i would take so many bribes if i was a judge. half my shit would be bribes. take bribes from the criminals until theyre too poor to do crime

wint
@dril

1014263539219955716

Ur Honor, The Jury Is Obviously Biased Against Me Because Theiyre Mad., And They're Butt Hurt, And They Post On Different Forums Than I Do

wint
@dril

140238110876368896

the army: forbidden from jacking off. ~99% kill shot rate
the mafia: encouraged to jack off. cant kill guys unless theyre tied to chairs

wint
@dril

1025573691827019776

the jduge orders me to take off my anonymous v mask & im wearing the joker makeup underneath it. everyone in the courtroom groans at my shit

wint
@dril

575121631846227968

let's all kick the BTK killer's ass, all of us who make the good tweets,. we've got to meet up and beat the BTK killer's ass and go on dates

wint
@dril

473710782681997312

please stop saying barnum & bailey is suing me for "stealing their clown routine". they are suing me for very serious and legitimate reasons

wint
@dril

481774929286004736

don't know why people think it's fair to call me "The Piss Judge" just because I pissed all over the floor of my courtroom that one time

wint
@dril

230710725688045569

mcgruff the crime dogs Crime Tip #888853: if a criminal makes you play a game of darts to save a hostage's life throw the darts at his Dick

wint
@dril

158236129823428608

i can only hope that when a kangaroo court of dipshits comes to haul me to prison that i have the grace and humility not to get mad at them

**wint**
**@dril**

629398540830142464

lets mix the jail and the zoo togehter and have whistles going off constantly so nothing can sleep and spray piss and glue around as a bonus

**wint**
**@dril**

2225319791189551104

just wasted an entire afternoon at the court house trying to copyright th e phrase "Trump look like a uncle"

**wint**
**@dril**

916868814415056896

"during tibetan sky burials theres always the risk that the birds will eat everything except your dick and that people will laugh at the dick" wlel, it's almost time to deliver grandma's eulogy. the perfect time to announce that i'm quitting my job at IBM and becoming a SuicideGirl

wint
@dril

215681546978459649

surfs up! *lies face down in a kiddy pool until death*

wint
@dril

15576151669870592

ive accepted that i will have to reincarnate into shitty microorganisms like 50 quadrillion times before i become something cool like an ant

wint
@dril

482992297550675968

i would really like to attend my grandsons funeral but at the same time i just want to sit in bed and explore my body with a peacock feather

wint
@dril

326386680015757312

priest plugs my coffin in at the end of the funeral. "MILLERTIME" lights up in neon on the side, desecrating my corspe & sending me to hell

wint
@dril

199317160059875328

informed by family that i wont be invited to anymore funerals if i dont develop a jawline, fix my fucked up voice, and fix my fucked up skin

wint
@dril

2192385993994448576

if your grave doesnt say "rest in peace" on it you are automatically drafted into the skeleton war

wint
@dril

361282749086175234

so long suckers! i rev up my motorcylce and create a huge cloud of smoke. when the cloud dissipates im lying completely dead on the pavement

wint
@dril

757914951868485632

Join us for "Goodbye Cathy: 34 Years Of Laughs", located in Pittsburgh's famous Motel 6 Rumpus Room, the event will conclude with my suicide

wint
@dril

21072215094

i truly hate winning the infamous "Darwin Award" by getting bombarded with artillery fire in the Super K-Mart parking lot

wint
@dril

755206152816852992

"first they ignore you
then they laugh at u
then you jack off & read posts for 30 years
then you die of pulmonary heart disease
then you Win"

#ReplaceMovieTitleWithCheese the n.w.o and the illuminati orchestrated katrina and colony collaspe || send paypal to BLOODTRUTH@yahoo.com

223891173385830401

not many good wiki leaks lately. was hoping Julian woudld find out which individual or agency keeps ripping the gutters off of my house

281084633142157312

FBI AGent: We have given u a new identity because of the death threats your bad posts get you. Youre Tim Crap now
Me (as Tim Crap now): Cool

521873409316487169

i just got word from cigarnet that the government has a secret vault full of #GUNS

368303879131127808

regardless of if he's real or not . can we please just talk about how much bigfoot sucks ass. what has he done with his life

983342291011194880

i destoryed my balls with uh, enhanced interrogation techniques sir

wint
@dril

546706030026293248

#5ReasonsIHateFacebook DIRTY GOVT TRICKS, CRIME CODES, THE 666 MICRO CHIP, BOROUGH COUNCILMAN "RODGE PETRIS" , WAR PLANET-- LOOK UM UP

wint
@dril

2286697556477750144

i have still not ruled out the possibility that the jellyfish i stepped on while collecting seashells at the beach was a False Flag

wint
@dril

3241975803953888928

some people say that area 51 is a jail for aliens. i say its where the army keeps their best guns

wint
@dril

5178533901275513601

vladimir Putin if youre reading this please grant me asylum like you did with snowdan. i too ,am constantly in hot water because of my posts

wint
@dril

4253468258190029504

mail 1000 envelopes addressed to "The Desert" and watch endless waves of government pawns march to their death #ANARCHY2012 #sand

wint
@dril

1714532660502978 57

FBI deemed my tool assisted glitch run of Mario Teaches Typing too dangerous for the public eye. the raw emotion has rendered my face purple

wint
@dril

1568799700257 38240

30+ YEARS OF CATHY ABRUPTLY HALTED-- LATEST VICTIM OF CORPORATE ELITE'S WAR AGAINST POPULIST INSUBORDINATION #OPPRESSION #BETRAYAL #ARTDEATH

wint
@dril

21062301173

"ey!! im walkin here" - me getting waterboarded by the us government

wint
@dril

3307955807 35500290

ufo themed wedding thwarted by sjw `s

wint
@dril

9791487060 91077632

the us government has its top men working day and night to invent a paper towel that is large enough to wrap me up and dispose of me

wint
@dril

463195199964213248

droid is filth. govt trick to ID and persecute civilians for $. real ID is 666 - thow all micro chips into the trash can. piss #IWantADroid

wint
@dril

15174111185608704

i receive a generous amount of funds from the US government, as they believe that my good tweets are an effectuive deterrent to masturbation

wint
@dril

455022203206389764

im crying because doctors banned the cure for low T again

wint
@dril

479663634747240448

if satan tries to put a microchip in my gun i will shoot him

wint
@dril

408428840755544064

*"u go through life thinking the man wears the diaper. but at what point does the diaper wear the man. #diapermaster"*

wint
@dril

the Police have stated that rubber neckers and looky loos trying to sneak a peek at the irradiated diaper on 295 will be blasted with poison

911687742521794561

wint
@dril

i sometimes wonder how shaken the AB/DL community would be if they found out i was injecting my diaper with saline solution instead of Shit

281815604225273857

wint
@dril

for the last time, Diaper is capitalized when referring to the lifestyle or state of mind, but not when referring to the physical object.

60036804929273856

wint
@dril

you have the right to remain Diapered. anything you shit can and will be held against you in a quart of piss

1485272968863670272

wint
@dril

i will tell you about the two types of diaper. there's the Functional diaper, worn inside the pants. and the Aesthetic diaper, worn outside.

657287245947379712

\*\*shooting bow & arrow into huge pile of discarded diapers piercing like five or six of them with each shot\* now that`s what i call Combos

wint
@dril

451205689344802817

god grant me the serenity 2 accept the Diapers i cant change, the courage to change the Diapers i can, & the wisdom to shit myself profusely

wint
@dril

193383023880847362

8 of the navy's finest men rappel into my quarters and change my diaper. i stumble towards the balcony and throw cans at their helicopter

wint
@dril

244146373941927936

review: koala kare diaper station with the fuckin bear on it. awful. sorry im not some size 0 model who can use this without it snapping off

wint
@dril

306071886494855168

indeed, i am Very Diapered right now, currently pairing a Pampers Cruiser with a quarter glass of Marcus Sinclair's Cape Cod November Ale

wint
@dril

139028125412626432

wint
@dril

"diapers are for animal at the zoo". nmever in my life have i seen a more ignorant comment written online and overlooked by the hitler media

3147664037208637444

wint
@dril

changing 500 tiny diapers on 500 disgusting rats #TheLifeIChose

87525947724664832

wint
@dril

dirty jobs man tcame to my house today with camera crew and a bunch of diapers. i said no

144753276192071170

wint
@dril

ever since i changed my gametap id from "diapermaster" to "CoolBryce" a world of doors have opened up to me.

19855284433

wint
@dril

well, at leas i have my dignity. *trrips over shoelace, somersaults itno 3500mph faceplant, pants and dirty diaper fly off ass across room*

12295173117

served thanksgivng turkey wearing diaper to family ; my coming out as a Wearer -- one thing im NOT thankful for is rudeness and betrayal

wint @dril

1372954311043399968

my 14beautiful geisha brides work together to change my preposterous 300 pound diaper. #mtvcribs

wint @dril

401250420040704011

Dont see whats so funny about me accidentaly getting a tattoo of a diaper, but by all means, dont let me stop the Circle Jerk. By all means,

wint @dril

8868370934854778888

i remark "mummies are made out of diapers" at the egypt museum. some cops jump out a sarcophagus and begin humping me as i roll on the floor

wint @dril

3147734431512698888

A MAD TYRANT has cracked the admin password for IRC chatroom #DiaperIsrael -- the entirety of DARKNET is in peril

wint @dril

2039806771741409288

**wint**
**@dril**

dear god. in all my years.... an ancient diaper perfectly preserved in amber-- no wait, its just some shitty caveman head. throw it back

178870574335004672

**wint**
**@dril**

every one must wear a free speech diaper to protest twitter deleting posts that say "Fuck the ecliopse" and "The eclipse is some fake shit"

899313725483692038

**wint**
**@dril**

TRYING TO RECONCILE MY STAUNCHLY SELF-DEPENDENT SMALL GOVERNMENT BELIEFS WITH MY CONSTANT NEED FOR DIAPER CHANGES

5190877072850945

**wint**
**@dril**

how about a diaper with belt loops. anyone

11386096913

**wint**
**@dril**

sick and tired of people assuming im taking a shit whenever i go to the bathroom,; while im actually just running my diaper under the sink

914559881000230913

wint
@dril

i left a diaper filled with pulled pork at 1 randomly selected radio shack in the united states. whoever finds it gets to #BringHomeTheBacon

481084779543031808

wint
@dril

i have been advised not to ascend to the spirit plane in my sissy dress and #diapers

15131259118

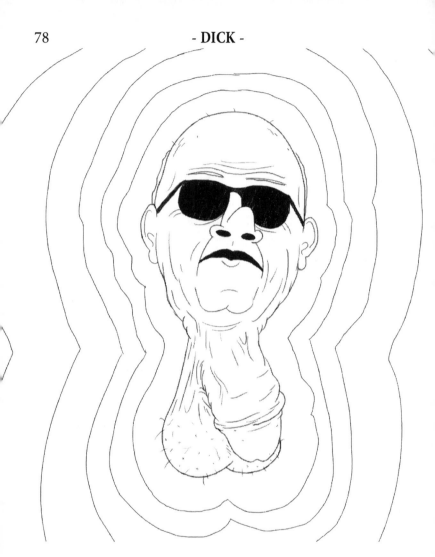

"*my dick sucks balls. pray for my dick*"

someday mankind will evolve beyond "jokes" and i'll be allowed to paint big ugly dicks all over my house without suffering derisive laughter

wint
@dril

350928998450208768

detective sherlock holmes examines my crass pud with a magnifying glass and calls it a piece of shit

wint
@dril

500491347535859713

this weeks "Mother Fucker" award goes to BabePigMovieMan for saying my dick looks "Crumpled up like a napkin"

wint
@dril

586552899288858624

i habve been banned from over 200 dating services for being upfront and honest about my rotten, barbed dick

wint
@dril

374881468352577536

YO *points to spinal cord on brain diagram* THATS THE BRAIN;S DICK

wint
@dril

179736293641682944

wint
@dril

thank you for emailing me the picture of the pillsbury doughboys dick while my dad and all my uncles were standing right behind me. Not

367337623573901313

wint
@dril

too much pressure from society saying we all got to learn how to self suck. iwill never self suck my dick and im unfollowing anyone who does

606120246450257920

wint
@dril

proudly announcing to the barber shop that i got through my entire haircut without screaming or touching my dick underneath the smock

552539658878722049

wint
@dril

i just sucked my own dick and got poisoned. no podcast tonight

369997365983195136

wint
@dril

me, begging and pleading with a turtle, telling it to spit out my dick , causing a scene at a miniature golf course and getting 911 called

119427984460484608

**wint**
@dril

my dick hits all the wrong notes and smells like newsPaper

514307822474248192

**wint**
@dril

*steps out on stage twirling a cane and accidentally hits self in the dick 100 times * AAAWGHHH

402672788575498240

**wint**
@dril

UNCLE: on sept 14 u posted "my dick is not all its cracked up to be." Explain yourself please
ME: its. a commentary on the economy actually,

670215924704653312

**wint**
@dril

inspirational... 86 year old man circumcised by doctors in Zaire... "It's never too late" "Blessed."

659511531051343872

**wint**
@dril

hm? whats that? my dick looks like bozo the clown's dick? listen punk. i know for a fact you have never seen bozo the clown's dick

355094691269722112

i hate it when my dick gets dredged in flour, egg and breadcrumbs, in that order

wint
@dril

900887673665200128

My dick is wearing a neck brace

wint
@dril

928533474323116032

need to know who wrote "Micropenis Kisser" on my barbeque grill, because if i actually ever kissed a micropenis i must inform my lips doctor

wint
@dril

231692346645946369

(poking head up from self suck) augh this tastes like dog shit (goes back for more)

wint
@dril

712213136863051776

how do people know how big their dicks are. is there an online quiz you can take

wint
@dril

579773899568766976

founnd a cicada skin stuck to my nefarious pud

wint
@dril

629698445297741825

dropped a mouthful of spaghetti on my dick just now

wint
@dril

891216607141404672

CLICK ON MY BIG DUMB DICK TO SUBSCRIBE TO MY USELESS NEWSGROUP

wint
@dril

21102190087

took failblog to court for putting puicture of my dick up, settled for $6. a victory, because im worht far less than that

wint
@dril

6934463314

i go outside for the rfirst time in 7 years and a biplane immediately shoots a chemtrail at my dick and makes it 2 inches shorter. typical

wint
@dril

660875546658775040

if iyou come on here talking to me about your penis, or saying unreasonable things about my penis, your account will be "Knocked down"

wint
@dril

884450115498504192

My dick looks like a cartoon character's

wint
@dril

397497505513865216

wringing my dick out like a sponge and letting all that gray water drip all over my bluesuede shoes

wint
@dril

857620926187405313

*kicks back and watches an algorithm remove all the circumcised people from my web ring* Huauha your fucked up dicks can't save you now

wint
@dril

377935701821505536

one, of, the , reasons, my, dick, is, not, good, is, because, there, are, stains, on, it,

wint
@dril

497859621252771840

my dick is satire

wint
@dril

3398792282773 95457

getting my pud Encrypted , like peter thiel

wint
@dril

9354257577231 85152

putting the vacuum on my dick until I stop
hearing crumbs go down the tube

wint
@dril

7171562816692 71552

saying "augh" out loud every single time
I move the phone away from my lap and
reveal to my self, my pud, which looks like a
coiled turd

wint
@dril

8451501567145 00097

we;ll its time for me to pick the scabs off of
what i not-so-affectionately refer to as my
"Fail Dick"

wint
@dril

13616331237

wint
@dril

tge nicest thing about me is i have excessively dry balls which basically start flaking apart like a piece of strudel whenever I walk around

596353717886156801

wint
@dril

my dick is a beak now

393636916618223616

"i think that in 2013 digimon otis was seirously convinced that they were going to change the name of gamestop to gameMosque"

the brief period in high school when DigimonOtis changed his name to BurgerKingOtis in an attempt to improve his image

wint
@dril

392341965162811392

"I believe the Egyptian people have no reason to replace their rightly instated leader with some sort of primitive pyramid god." DigimonOtis

wint
@dril

31132737670746112

i fully intend to topple the DigimonOtis empire via a coordinated campaign of viral folk songs bolstered by my partnership w/ Bob Evans Inc.

wint
@dril

364913729881649152

images leaked of WildArmsGarret , trusted consigliere of DigimonOtis, taking a bath in one of those old fashioned metal wash tubs

wint
@dril

727186362982653953

i am truly devastated to announce that DigimonOtis is in a coma after getting his arm trapped underneath a beatmania cabinet #PrayForOtis

wint
@dril

244157472863043584

(reading my latest death threat ) "from the desk of DigimonOtis..." this is bullshit. digimonotis has never owned a desk

**wint**
**@dril**

5303969851999951872

digimonotis thought octomom was the bad guy in spider man 2

**wint**
**@dril**

4133935230611161984

this one time-- me, DigimonOtis, and EpicWayne tried to open up a barbershop together, but the plan fell through due to my fear of hair

**wint**
**@dril**

1488683868420833330

i often disagree with DigimonOtis, but his efforts to keep Sharia Law out of the donkey kong 64 wiki are much needed in this wolrd of danger

**wint**
**@dril**

8928254828147711203

@DigimonOtis Fuck yourself

**wint**
**@dril**

2613749611120333824

digmon otis once mistook a beached toilet for a dolphin egg

wint
@dril

372887805891842048

"*eating a single Dorito on a bed of Jasmine Rice*"

ALERT: don pablos app has malware that photo shops your pics to make it look like youre crying & sends them to every girl on my contact list

wint
@dril

913826802702979073

(dismissing waitress handing me the check with a hand wave) no thank you. i dont believe in any of that

wint
@dril

814070430269054976

the guys who make steaks should make all of them "grade A" steak,. ythese guys have been making this shit for 1000 years, no more excuses

wint
@dril

906634585823498240

when it comes to eating things at restaurants i love the shit that is "Fresco"

wint
@dril

901863993224155136

if you want the real bargains during boys night out... gotta go with the Children's menu... every time

wint
@dril

636944880766451712

**wint**
**@dril**

CHEF: mon signor!! leaving the tails on the shrimp is good! it is tre bien
ME: Im going to nuke you with live ammo. Im the guy from the crow

6431876783857336 32

**wint**
**@dril**

(insufferably) It's pronounced. "Bloomin Onion." The 'g' is silent.

7749740771 90696963

**wint**
**@dril**

now im a man whos been eating his fuckin spaghetti, i tell you what for damn sure. tghat being said, toilet paper needs to be about 3x wider

5190744077810073 60

**wint**
**@dril**

you d o not have to tip the waiter if you say "Thank You" more than 50 times, over the course of the meal

8758976333568778 24

**wint**
**@dril**

i got a big wet piece of corn and the cob in my bindle and i cant wait to run it over with my truck after im done chewing on it

4890664887754465 28

the famous time-tested classic, the philly cheesesteak, has become Sexualized by greed

wint
@dril

782428918615773184

everyone loves it when i go to their parties and mix all the whips together (cool wip, reddi wip, miracle whip etc) like a fucking shit head

wint
@dril

798861055036366848

#InterestingDevelopments:do not purhcase Hatfield Quality Meats as they contain a rare pigment alloy that turrns your skeleton bones black

wint
@dril

2535798760

i have proof that my care taker has been tricking me into eating delicious home cooked meals by hiding them in wads of peanut butter

wint
@dril

554205717822193664

im thinking now, about how pissed off i'd get if i was dining at a 4-star restaurant and the waiter came out 100% nude. do not do that shit

wint
@dril

996462126452609025

llove to look at a big slice of meatloaf and say "Damn it's good"

wint
@dril

444091934962089984

me & khryler are drawing up plans for a family restaurant with damn good jeans nailed to the walls. we will call it the hard rock jeans cafe

wint
@dril

391048332094607360

frowning while the entire waitstaff of California pizza kitchen sings "happy birthday" to me, looking like a lump of shit in a neckbrace

wint
@dril

768799870664802304

(folloiwng the waiter to his car) Sir. Sir. Can you confirm or deny that the Southwestern Chipotle Chicken Paninis here are "Chef Inspired"

wint
@dril

947750858032369669

im going to have to put the tiny padlock next to my username until people stop oppenly disparaging the Food Pyramid

wint
@dril

482994138942828544

fucking nobel laureates screaming at each other about the current state of Juggalo Love in the handicap stall at dennys

wint
@dril

1570995509963038872

"[Tipping] is...the last refuge of toads" - Thomas Jefferson
"Do not tip the waitress" - Monroe
"i dont tip bitch. Reblog this" - John Adams

wint
@dril

513747429477580800

downloading shit loads of counterfeit papa john coupons through unsecure wifi net works

wint
@dril

849650642696187904

to the longhorn steakhouse which refused to serve me: a bib most certainly counts as a shirt

wint
@dril

486645428667289601

HIBACHI MAN AT @Benihana__ - WILL NOT PREPARE KRAFT MACARONI AS REQUESTED - THIS IS THE ONLY THING I CAN EAT - IM VERY ILL

wint
@dril

1272256511734046473

imbecile goes viral after telling tgifridays waiter that his caesar dressing is "too spicy"

wint
@dril

640728610807095296

Waiter! Oh Waiter! Yes, I`d like to know if I have earned any CashBack Reward`s™ with the purchase of my farm fresh miniature cucumber plate

wint
@dril

750328149485977600

absolutely pounding a zip lock bag of cut up hot dogs in the portle potty

wint
@dril

868558649760915457

sees another grown man eating cheerios off his table at the restaurant, gives him the restaurant cheerio nod

wint
@dril

419333310318252033

thank you inventor of bibs. every one else, off a cliff

wint
@dril

544256595136622592

whenever i see someone eating without a bib i laugh and shake my head. beucase i just know they're going to fuck their shirt up with stains

wint
@dril

4010723081035561217

sipping some campbell's chunky soup from flask in coat pocket

wint
@dril

438437583652417536

im not tipping any more waiters until the facts come in, regarding Putin

wint
@dril

857622319593914368

theyer renovating my hard rock cafe.. just saw a mover man drag two crates of live rattlers inside..has Hard Rock gone TOo wild?? No F'n Way

wint
@dril

78281705345130496

each 'Ridge' in your crinkle-cut potato chip costs 4 gallons of precious slave blood to create and adds a satisfying "Cruntch" to every bite

wint
@dril

636908091112574976

**wint**
**@dril**

helping the waitstaff by wiping the table down with the same disgusting napkin that I just used to sop up all the bullshit off my face

7131420515761143872

**wint**
**@dril**

consumeralert: at least one butterball turkey has been stuffed with the shrunken head of an assassinated african dictator. be care full.

6085811260

**wint**
**@dril**

"Ah!! Lunchtime, Boys!" i snort several lines of Hamburger Helper, tilt my head back and shake with unbearable agony as my head turns purple

334707291590901760

**wint**
**@dril**

Waiter, by the advice of the Chicago Tribune Id like a Dash of Ground Cumin on my Farm Fresh Egg. Oh! Too much! I withdraw this transaction,

618904901381324800

**wint**
**@dril**

casually discarding styrofoam container filled with buffalo wing remnants into the passing stroller of a baby

474226745395003392

I'm Sorry For Raising Cain At The Out Back Steak House Even Though It's Still Bullshit That They Refuse To Serve Me A Plate Of Just Croutons

wint
@dril

337825108376825856

1989: the fall of the berlin wall is celebrated, historically revered
2016: i tear down the sneeze guard at old country buffet and get Booed

wint
@dril

734307632375336960

seeing the words "Farm Fresco" on a billboard and having to pull the fuck over from becoming Overstimulated

wint
@dril

916555643900874752

i would really like to wipe this spilled chili off of me but all my towels are fucked up right now

wint
@dril

522207533248040961

ah.. the perfect Souffle! cant wait to dig in to t(*EVERY PIPE IN MY HOUSE EXPLODES AT THE SAME TIME, COVERING ME IN SHIT AND BOILING WATER*

wint
@dril

773559859287584771

"did we end sars yet. good job every one, if we did"

well im going to keep this brief. i overexerted myself while responding to emails and got put up in the hospital. i basically need lungs now

wint
@dril

3771104270627446785

if you feel uncomfortable reading about my balls infection, click X. if not, pour a good big beer and let my feed take you to another world,

wint
@dril

310895315781816320

chiropracty is real and it works on swords also.

wint
@dril

38767557062168576

hidden camera prank doctor: we got your xrays back. Looks like your brain has been replaced by bugs
me (oblivious): please let me g go home

wint
@dril

535443344244342784

oh nothin, i was just buying some ear medication for my sick uncle... *LOWERS SHADES TO LOOK YOU DEAD IN THE EYE* who's a Model by the way,

wint
@dril

197502223226384387

dont u dare step foot into my dojo until youve read oprah's blog post about east asian nutrigenomics and their remarkable immunity to autism

wint
@dril

1988770096639011696

DICK DOCTOR: have you been using protection
ME: yes. i put an entire towel in my ass

wint
@dril

561243989786243072

you know what. im going to just come out and say it. i think that we should let the geico geckco go into hospitals & entertain the bedridden

wint
@dril

5738534490681146688

raise Hell to end workplace discrimination against men who suffer from PL (Pube Loss). force my boss to pay due tribute to my pristine mound

wint
@dril

308601774216978432

Asthmatic Blogger Expo Ruiend By Very Dusty Man

wint
@dril

1112338499970790400

extremely getting a uti by usnig the same shirt i used to wipe my dogs mouth to wipe piss off of my dick

wint
@dril

1001481184403185665

no you see, if you look closely at this drawing he put a face on the sun. clearly this child is autistic

wint
@dril

134268900559949824

yo!! check THIs out *reveals a sickening green bruise spanning entire stomach and partial left thigh*

wint
@dril

16706700321

you are treated to the serene visage of a waterfall cascading against the rocks. the camera pans out and its me vomiting all over my balls

wint
@dril

360789347068420096

SCIENTIST INVENT VACCINE THAT CURES AND CAUSE AUTISM AT THE SAME TIME. THE ULTIMATE HIGH

wint
@dril

19261369536

donate $78 to the " micropenis" awareness fund for a orange micropenis ribbon to show your support for micropenis. i have it

wint
@dril

6535702185

#red for aids tuesday i will guarantee a 5% decrease in worldwide hiv infections by kkeeping my filthy dick out of the pacific ocean

wint
@dril

6230072462

do not be alarme.d the repulsive green hue of my dick and legs and stomach is merely a side effect of fucking bags of wet grass constantly

wint
@dril

2460091202976428032

they were goign to preserve my brain but they decided it would be a waste of a jar. they instead used the jar to store a massive piss sample

wint
@dril

5311137957336735744

surgury to become japanese. Surgeruy to become Japanese

wint
@dril

4804100058602594305

"*i call evbery four-legged animal I see a dog and I am correct more often than not so I will never stop*"

gov bans pit bull fighting because they are scared of the power pits can achieve by gaining BOth strengh & wisdom in the barbwire gauntlet

wint
@dril

1634664620051783368

@thescienceguy the natural course of life dictates that by 9000AD hte entire human race will have either died off or evolved into pitbulls

wint
@dril

245319390394978304

the large hadron collier will never detect the higgs boson particle. the only purpose it has is to rile dogs up

wint
@dril

1799733247637471232

two men fighting inside of a dog igloo

wint
@dril

175463619516043266

do they make those cones that dogs wear after surgery for people? ?? i need to stop spitting on my dick

wint
@dril

28817814060

i dress as a medieval knight and pummel my metal body with cymbals to get all 59 of my pit dogs riled up before i fling lawn chairs at them

wint
@dril

163469423716478976

the reason i poured vinegar all over TwistedKenneth's bike ramp is because he made a gross joke about piercing my dog`s nipple

wint
@dril

250265253907136512

whats the job where you dress up like a michelin man and get attacked by vicious dogs. anyway thats the thing i spent $800000 at college for

wint
@dril

494255011656785921

u got 1 side saying dogs have paws & the other side saying dogs have hooves..then me, the guy who cuts thru the BS, saying they have Niether

wint
@dril

768406496031993856

the reason dogs constatntly bark at me everywhere i go is that dogs are animals that were born in shit and are a bullshit animal in history.

wint
@dril

240324614201421824

TODAY WE EXPLORE THE CONTRIBUTIONS THAT WOMEN HAVE MADE TO ARENA PITBULL DEATHMATCH

wint
@dril

297345480134889473

i love to build illegal temples around town. i love scrubbing my pitbull down with big piles of soap bubbles. i love to fuss and raise shit.

wint
@dril

350440888549380096

proposed mural of Dr. martin luther king breastfeeding a pitbull wrapped in us flag REJECTED by town "Fucking" hall #DeathEarth #EarthDeath

wint
@dril

2148409206113364864

@DogBountyHunter what if you sprayed a can of pepper mace directly at my ass. what wouald happen. also congrats on season 2 or whatever

wint
@dril

161635999267565569

HOW MUCH IS $500 IN DOG YEARS

wint
@dril

122724270114734080

**wint**
@dril

if i ever get Crucified i would like it to be on my official warhammer 40,000 surfboard while my all my pitbulls bark at me

2199780104441416704

**wint**
@dril

if id known he was planning on using it to wipe his dogs shitty mouth i wouldve never allowed XenoMarcus to borrow my monogrammed neckbrace

2394216962710691184

**wint**
@dril

dead certainly., if my pit bulls could speak... they would say "please, please increase my power"

6498536282248314888

**wint**
@dril

@MiracleGro MIRACLE GROW GAVE MY DOG HEART WORM

213459616586153984

**wint**
@dril

always take my stagecoach full of pit bulls to the Range . because my girls love to watch me shoot

621296903225896960

"*in hell you are forced to smoke weed*"

if anyone knows what to do if you accidentally swallow an entire cigar while running on the treadmill please contact StogieLad@Yahoo.com

wint
@dril

286264467313029120

in order to alleviate the stress of having to witness sub par content on my feed, several of my followers have suggested that i try "Heroin"

wint
@dril

921288451978350593

" snorting a line of coke up my big ass "

wint
@dril

7712125027303554688

i am actually the first guy who came up with the "aliens who smoke weed" joke, back in 2011

wint
@dril

504152864642859008

i went to arizona accompanied by two desert goblins and smoked spirit leaf out of a human stomach

wint
@dril

375825102048219136

to stand nude before a group of middle aged italian mob bosses and have them obnoxiously berate your dick while smoking cigars

wint
@dril

41450578584420352

a fuckin.. rat eating a slice of pizza?? damn,. the guy who filmed this must have gbeen smoking weed.

wint
@dril

657256347050889216

my name is Destyn. i build crossbows and sell weed to all your dads and im 15

wint
@dril

515701343735283712

once again its up to me to take the high road. while everyones making jokes of the fat weed smoker mayor ill be whipping myself in his honor

wint
@dril

462237916463235072

thinking of becoming a "Pipes" dipshit

wint
@dril

848747963174334464

**wint**
**@dril**

obama's ban on clove cigarettes has affected
me Spiritually

7867580425

**wint**
**@dril**

oculus allows you to smoke wii remote like
a cigar and blow heaps of smoke in celebs
faces

610553956826226688

**wint**
**@dril**

my cigar rival just posted another vid....
time to leave the kids with nana , switch it to
hell mode and outsmoke this BAStard

3196799428897721856

**wint**
**@dril**

even if youre not a comics guy, i woud
fully recommend grabbin a cigar
and experiencing Blondie's 948-strip
"BENEDICTION" arc in one sitting

2230174002479218592

**wint**
**@dril**

despite this being the 1 day that allows the
legal use of "Ghanja", i will isntead opt to
absorb the celebrated works of Foxworthy &
Engvall

3256375375550983169

people think people smoke weed because it tastes good. well i'm here to tell you that people like it because it gets you drunk asap

wint
@dril

512880449514127360

jacking off.. (lights cigarette, takes a big smoke of it) ..i s a Zero Sum fallacy. a jesters game

wint
@dril

668764374065135616

i want to be responsible for getting carly rae jespen into cigarettes just so i can be sure she's taking a christian brand

wint
@dril

233570497361743873

just set up My Quicken Loans accounts for a whole small ecuadorian village, entirely on chrystal meth. keep doing your little posts though .

wint
@dril

938312377648467968

"*its no secret that i sometimes have to scold my hare brained followers rirght in their goofy fucking faces to keep them in line*"

just me again reminding all of you seriousyl dumb motherfuckers to get your daily sperm count. some of you are walking around with weak cum.

wint
@dril

472162701486346241

DUMBASS: SHut the fuck up
THE WISE MAN: No you shut the fuck up

wint
@dril

879453684987572226

doing my favorite " Shit head " activity, kissing a cactus after being fooled nby a mirage

wint
@dril

904020515899277313

im dumb as a slab of turds, and i am Here for it

wint
@dril

949907037315624961

they should make dunce caps that have positive reaffirming words on them, like "speed demon" or "Wolf"

wint
@dril

484719255997280257

imagine how fucked uop it would be to have a brain and be able to form thoughts

wint
@dril

513403807481737216

getting my pussy hammered like a dumb ass

wint
@dril

888616125482795009

fucked up my hand while trying to pry open a jar of cherries with a Shuriken

wint
@dril

944640058132398080

i feel, as I, over time, become even more of a Dumb Ass, i am able to consume web-based content and Media at increasingly Blistering speeds,

wint
@dril

784440328933761025

(ddumb ass, squinting at the tv, struggling to comprehend "The Flintstones") why are they wearing those outfits

wint
@dril

6517357015166627968

completing my "Dip Shit" look by donning a humongous bib with a picture of a sailboat on it

wint
@dril

967465536178270208

 The one thing that I am truly the most sick of dealing with online is Ignorance Likers .

wint
@dril

366353621421531137

 i know im a dumb ass for expecting a serious response from the chucklefuck brigade, but can someone please tell me if im circumcised or not

wint
@dril

628527051016777728

 sometimes i wonder what this place would be like if i wasnt around to call bull shit on all the jokers... probably the 9/11 crater but worse

wint
@dril

513438584339464193

 im sorry but, when you people reply to my posts with things like "Fuck you" and "Fuck your Account" it makes me look like a real dumb ass

wint
@dril

906069846097629184

"buy shares in the Markets. i have a really good feeling about the markets"

i refuse to partake in any hot black friday deals today out of respect for all the dead folks on the benghazi strip #shopping #deals #prayer

wint
@dril

271908120886919169

it pains me to announce that as of april 5th, 2018, The Economist has severed ties with "Da Ass Fucka"

wint
@dril

9820500041065037824

in 2023 an unassuming fat man will become the official currency of the united states. the economy will collapse because theres only 1 of him

wint
@dril

286844794360188929

surefire investment: Saline. everyone i know is injecting a lot of it into their dicks. THat's, "Saline". Surefire investment. Locked down.

wint
@dril

410404257934761985

i believe that jade healm 15, and the markets going haywire, youve got a "Witch's Brew" of bull shit

wint
@dril

636915713635188736

THHEYRE GOING TO MAKE A LOT OF FUCKING BUILDINGS IN TH NEXST COMING YEARS SO MAKE SURE TO INVEST A LOT OF MONEY IN WOOD

wint
@dril

511831273363738624

if you see me dragging a compass through the sand, i'm conducting Market Analysis and must not be distracted

wint
@dril

217719972858830849

seems like to me that in this foul economy the only thing "On the Up and Up" is the damn gas prices, thath we all gotta break the bank for .

wint
@dril

652197535247921152

96 year old man goe's back to kindergarten after losing ihs job at the chemical weapons factory due to Gas Prices and the Economy #InspireMe

wint
@dril

855547214944493575

thinking about getting the dow jones back on track, simply by making a few phonecalls. but certain people have been a bitch to me, so i wont

wint
@dril

959646059126550528

wint
@dril

Food $200     Data $150     Rent $800
Candles $3,600          Utility $150
someone who is good at the economy please
help me budget this. my family is dying

384408932061417472

wint
@dril

because of the RECESSION, "Ice Capades"
has been cancleled and replaced by
SHITcapades and PISScapades. just kidding

10571557565

wint
@dril

sell shares in pond demons. i;m
disappointed in pond demons

226176408257429504

wint
@dril

executing some advanced high-risk
transactions on the Markets. trading my ass
medicine for dick medicine

977935068709744642

wint
@dril

i am skeptical of the concept "Too Big To
Fail" mainly because i am extremely big and
i fail constantly

387760174401732608

" 'Soda is back' Only at Mcdonald"

**wint**
**@dril**

the blue thumnbtacks on this map indicate concentrations of high 月(luna) energy, the red ones are all the panera breads ive been banned from

2163749680936509444

**wint**
**@dril**

check out the new "Five For Five" offer at mc donalds... thats Five soda's for five bucks "Or your money back"

786885830375829504

**wint**
**@dril**

i hand the chipotle cashier my card. "i support indie" with a photograph of me winking. she looks up and sees me winking in real life also.

378337320971169794

**wint**
**@dril**

yea i totally deserve to be put on the sex offender registry cause i got caught taking pictures of my feet at fiveguys burger and fries. Not

250218099473805312

**wint**
**@dril**

im the guy at mcdonalds who decides which states the offers are not valid in, an d i get more death threats than god

846489221942722560

free mustard offered at burger king...
genius?? or a "Beta Move"

wint
@dril

827895544295092229

stepping into fiveguys hq, just listing
hundreds of brand new chef-inspired value
combos off the top of my head. Boom. just
like that. 1 2 3

wint
@dril

1008448265237549058

#secretturnon pointing to a picture of
Grimace at mcdonalds and asking the
cashier "Who Is That Awful Purple Man?"

wint
@dril

17721076557545473

"I envision a dining experience tailored
specifically for the public masturbator.
Therein lies the Soul of the Roy Rogers
brand."-Roy Rogers

wint
@dril

4365625742312284416

2013: burger king creates "The Doritos
Whopper" 2021: orson scott card writes
"The Doritos Novel" 2035:removed from
matrix. no more doritos

wint
@dril

185772916623941632

for $0.39 extra the burger king man will write "yu-gi-oh" on your hamburger in magic marker

**wint**
@dril

22456957331832832

they should put slot machines in the mc donalds. i want to win baby

**wint**
@dril

903037395012128768

hey @BurgerKing your trays dont fit in the fuckin trash cans. i am a CFO in real life and an oversight like this would cost me my Nuts .

**wint**
@dril

767400789736316928

by calling them "Stackers" instead of quesadillas, taco bell is legally allowed to fill them with 49% bird shit

**wint**
@dril

993006582874169345

i can eat as much burger king i want w/o geting fat, sorta like how babies can breathe underwater because theyre pure

**wint**
@dril

16769519190

i sacrifice my most valuable gift card to the ocean to quell the intensity of the raging waters. forgive me, saladworks .

**wint**
**@dril**

2732582025425100081

now that i'm unemployed I can finally weave an intricate fan universe based on the chick fil a cows who are always holding the signs up

**wint**
**@dril**

4209207332259755808

i walked in on two cops touching each other's badges in the unisex bathroom at saladworks and got a coupon from complaining about the ordeal

**wint**
**@dril**

3897607333354815488

i call upon familiars david blaine & criss angel to help me discretely wash this pocket pussy in the soda fountain at the peiwei asian diner

**wint**
**@dril**

4049922908566652800

lunch paraphernalia spilling out of the footwell of my car as i pull up to my old high school to steal footballs

**wint**
**@dril**

9930147841310433330

"*as a Parent.. the thought of somebody attacking my sons with some sort of weapon, is just not good to me*"

i have trained my two fat identical sons to sit outside of my office and protect my brain from mindfreaks by meditating intensely

**wint**
@dril

401469603903049729

i am a Gentleman's Son and i deserve the big gravy boat

**wint**
@dril

439501841366523904

its true. my father owned slaves in the 1980s but he has since apologized & been forgiven with love and support. he's a nice man now.

**wint**
@dril

576449474073108480

TODAY WE EXPLORE THE PROVEN INTELLECTUAL ADVANTAGE OF CHILDREN WHO HAD GENERAL HOSPITAL FANFICTION READ TO THEM IN THE WOMB

**wint**
@dril

297353230097186816

listen son, if someone calls you a horses ass, you look him in the eye and tell him "horses asses are actually incredibly strong, and clean"

**wint**
@dril

5154897663188829568

**wint**
@dril

my father banned me from taking shits after 8:00pm until i was 19 and this instilled within me a sense of morality and honor and respect

3149618384481894 40

**wint**
@dril

my dimwit sons love it when i drop them off at the car dealership for 7 hours while i cruise around for bargain's

4516451662823587 84

**wint**
@dril

ilove the idea of beating the shit out of my Son's rival's dad at the little league game with a suitcase full of cash

8523730903445544 97

**wint**
@dril

im 14 year s old and im already more psychic than my dad

3488509379153756 17

**wint**
@dril

plaese help my loathsome son find a professional who will tattoo the cheesecake factory logo onto his chest with no backtalk or jokes

5160248315829288 96

i can not catch a break folks. my 78 yr old son has been pissing into the boiler some how and making our home smell like a reptile enclosure

wint
@dril

788416187285864449

for every child you don't circumcise i am going to circumcise myself 3 times

wint
@dril

403727797396316160

today's the day that i put on my high heel cowboy boots & stomp the shit out of the fake plastic son that my father raised before i was born

wint
@dril

284147587441885184

grown man's ass surgically transplanted onto his son. final wish of a dying father

wint
@dril

231685930451345409

AAUh..!! Yeah. Lets all gang up on the guy who gives his children Steroids, just because he has a different opinion. Fucking idiots.

wint
@dril

657443529778724864

(carrrying a huge polkadotted bindle, looking like a dumb ass , shoes completely untied) Mother.. Father... Im leaving home to join the cops

wint
@dril

817542968764747776

i am taking my 34-year-old son into town to buy him his very first pair of clip-on suspenders and we are both very excited

wint
@dril

3424477360141271O5

everoy father's day my dad would take me out on a picnic, and he always filled our picnic basket with dirt, because dirt is the shit of God

wint
@dril

2145784431147423745

DAD: i just heard on t he news that teens are taking the "Kick My Ass" challenge. please dont do this
ME: you have no power over me, old man

wint
@dril

838195261067386880

surprise, dad. while you were witnessing the pennsylvania state lottery i tried on all your work gloves and they looked very handsome on me

wint
@dril

409176164075196416

**wint**
**@dril**

bougt a bottle of "liquid ass" to teach my stepdad a lesson but i consumed the entire bottle by mistake. now i drink "liqiud ass" on the reg

431198601276977153

**wint**
**@dril**

please pray for my sons Thursten and Gorse who have just glued themselves to a curtain,

546775065875185664

**wint**
**@dril**

i will pay a jpeg specialist up to $500 to put a black bar over the ass & pussy of my beloved rottweiler before i send the pic to my father.

353309343808102401

**wint**
**@dril**

my name is "hubo" now and not even my dad and all my uncles can change it back to "greg" no matter how many xboxs they step on

247894767285981184

**wint**
**@dril**

a father says to his 3 sons, "i love you all but I must fulfill my destiny as the Wind. goodbye" then he turns into the wind as his sons cry

156768229702897664

used the last remaining amount of my spirit force to transform mny daughter into a mana blade so that she will never cry again #AFathersPain

wint
@dril

292396774373597184

my son has been combing his hair without permission. how do i cope with the pain

wint
@dril

4305355527356313601

father wont stop opening my amazon boxes—How to proceed? (Self,Legal) TOP VOTED: put a live wire in his car & light his ass up. Cook his ass

wint
@dril

922426111920885760

"*im the guy who asked the baten kaitos forum if i should bring a condom to hooters*" cant wait til my teeth fall out so i can get those new gamer dentures that all the chatrooms are screaming about

**wint
@dril**

494998223912579072

alright now. just checking to see if there's any interest in a livestream of me speed running this entire bottle of hunts tomato ketchup

**wint
@dril**

381820871523852289

straight up-- im not here to make friends. im not here to socialize. im here because this is the only professional Mr. Bucket league in town

**wint
@dril**

274751350015922176

legally obligated to go door to door and inform neighbors of sex offender status but this is a good opportunity to sell my custom Gamecube's

**wint
@dril**

256004583871086592

1936: alan turing invents the computer and is persecuted for being gay.
2006: s. miyamoto invents the Wii and is persecuted for being Casual

**wint
@dril**

2331880639144889216

"Are Game's The Da Vinci Of The Modern Age" the interrogator barks. "What If Super Mario Was Real Life" he slaps the suspect across the face

wint
@dril

247328939326963714

the jerk off who told my autistic son that sega of america exploded needs to come forward so i can crush his neck betwext my Perfect thighs

wint
@dril

68055727922626560

if e3 does NOT #ShowUsTheGames, KeyBladeWalter, "Epic" Wayne Briggs and I will engage in disciplined self-immolation on the disgusting floor

wint
@dril

341933739523325954

how to convert ouija board to xbox controller using only a dead gamer

wint
@dril

122727219255709696

MetalGearEric: You are being tried in the court of gamers for calling Ninja Gaiden "Weiner Gaiden", even though it is not called that at all

wint
@dril

350946126272282626

how dare you fuck with me. how dare you fuck with me , on the year of Luigi

**wint**
**@dril**

348547842761170944

dont really care if my gaming chamber has black Mold all over it.. ill just curpstomp pubbies with my shirt pulled up over my nmose

**wint**
**@dril**

474171401168240640

me and TekkenChauncey banned from red lobster after getting into scuffle over gradius canon & becoming tangled in decorative fishing net

**wint**
**@dril**

159400873640996865

gentlemen, i implore you not to miss the Gamer's Challenge, wherein i will complete donkey kong countyr 3 (italian vrsn) without crying

**wint**
**@dril**

207489541119021058

haivng the xbox controller vibrate in my lap for 14 hours a day has rendered me sterile , low - t , and betagender

**wint**
**@dril**

528076887688740864

@Battlefield man named "Garth_Turds" has bene following me to every map and yelling "hitler" . Claims hes a mod. Get rid of him

wint
@dril

1353241088073441 28

@Battlefield user "Garth_Turds" jusr read my address online , except replacing the name of my town with "Toilet". my daughters are crying

wint
@dril

1353846293802639 36

@Battlefield User "Garth_Turds" still has not been banned. He's an utter nuisance. He's also using some kind of hack to make himself louder

wint
@dril

1353872511474196 49

@Battlefield "Garth_Turds" on here calling console fanboys the N-word. I ask you Garth, why is it that you're playing the PS3 version then?

wint
@dril

1402954844420177 92

@Battlefield once again, user "Garth_Turds" is running amok on this server, reading off a list of religions and making fart sounds w/ mouth

wint
@dril

1356830907471052 80

**wint**
@dril

@Battlefield The longer we both draw out this "Garth_Turds" debacle, the more foolish the both of us look.

1358306508748881192

 **wint**
@dril

i love haivng my face and head spit shined by army men while i am trying to play rpgs professionally and efficiently in my beanbag chair

515472991229325314

 **wint**
@dril

sorry oprah fanboys, but the Oprah MMORPG is a buggy mess, hasn't been patched in 7 years, and i regret playing it daily since i was a child

270876885871902722

 **wint**
@dril

little known fact: the e3 gaming conference is considered the holy grail of the public urination community

196682174357966848

 **wint**
@dril

id absolutely love to move to LA with my model g.friend & start my film career, but all my pre-orders at game stop would certainly be fucked

535430675391057920

the clown nose on my dick is there because im more susceptible to infection since my wii bowling accident, iddiot. no more hateful messages

wint
@dril

41575164588199936

me and my fat cousin are gonna tackle e3 gonzo style with a series of choreographed blogs an;d im rolling out a face book for gamers.

wint
@dril

16317729958

"my mario tip: Anything is possible in the world of Mario." - my mario tip

wint
@dril

4964033896l4264320

if you see a man in a fawkes mask walking down the highway with a sign that says "Gamestop: Power to the Players" that's me and i need water

wint
@dril

381474795310702592

im here to tell you that even with 8 kid,s, 6 dogs, debilitating rickets & a filthy waterlogged home, that its still possible to be a Gamer

wint
@dril

678619531389050880

my priceless stradivarius gaming keyboard...
fcovered in policeman urine

wint
@dril

447452314459447296

*sees the e3 logo on a website, tthrows
head back and screams the word "Epic"
before immediately defaulting to aberrant
emotionless state*

wint
@dril

475890472599056384

look, im not saying that martin luther king
jr was a gamer. that would be ludicrous. im
simply saying that if games had existed at
the time,

wint
@dril

830105130104127490

im uploading a "let's play" vid of me getting
stuck between the walls of my house and
getting all tangled up in the insulation and
shit

wint
@dril

171844570441719809

The Moderation and Administrative Staff
of the Star Fox Strategy and Technique
Discussion Boards DOES NOt encourage its
users to crank off,

wint
@dril

891209132727992320

wint
@dril

a reasonable compromise, would be to let the ISPs track our Gaming & reward more net neutraility to guys who get the most headshots & combos

9342360350301102O8

wint
@dril

DIVORCE GURU: gaming is a right, not a privilege. remember that always.
ME: Thank you divorce guru

6137377538434949I3

wint
@dril

#e3rumors a stodgy executive wil get on stage, spread his legs, and officially "give birth" to the new xbox. millions will detest this stunt

34I647405533515776

wint
@dril

exclusive footage obtained of Roger Ebert playing a sega and crying . we do nto forgive. we do not forget. this is Wikileaks. expect us.

I2678381244

wint
@dril

ive beenn using Confidence and Self Esteem lately, to get unprecedented deals on discarded promotional displays at game stop

754324549538312I92

mlg streamer "BeastModeCosby" loses geforce sponsorship after allegedly using a performance enhancing bed pan

wint
@dril

960956882985934849

sorry, all. "Let's Play: Pissrealms 2D: Part 314" has been postponed indefinitely, due to an injury i sustained while taking off my shirt

wint
@dril

199475827988103168

will e3 have designated crying booths. im sick of crying in the bathroom where people shit.

wint
@dril

475487859064184832

no. my bumper sticker of beautiful intergalactic bounty hunter Samus Aran saying "Im Autistic" couldnt have been the reason my car was towed

wint
@dril

309786720524709888

(after hearing the library has games , i arrive at the front desk, disguised as a non-gamer) er.. im here for some.. book's

wint
@dril

603976442494476288

wint
@dril

mother fucker calling himself Elmer Fudd on the CS server, NEed I remind you that, on the show, Elmer Fudd's Kill Count is essentially Zero?

880132028313866241

wint
@dril

thinking about taking all of the logs out of my fire place and using it as a gamer cave

985514064523735041

wint
@dril

tried to make an fps in the 90s but i only got as far as naming the difficulty levels "YA MOMMAS BOY", "PUKE" and "TURN THE GAME OFF DIPSHIT

5695236229907420674

wint
@dril

im a millionair and im going to pay blizzardgames $9.9bil on the stipulation that they put pornos in diabo 3

7595375266

wint
@dril

DAD: your baby brothers missing, please put down the controller. help us find him
ME: Did u read the news. Gaming is a legitinmate hobby now

505097444011806720

The Vagina Monologues, But For Gamers

wint
@dril

9681941273881168192

the show wife Swap but for gaming set ups

wint
@dril

1005978450086199296

The Dick Head On Team Chat Whose Smoke Detector Needs A New Battery: Does any one in here know how to fedex a pit bull

wint
@dril

991034043545288705

just indignantly threw $799 gamer keyboard into koi pond because i got pissed off by the craze that is sweeping the nation known as Planking

wint
@dril

622809162016120832

i have spent the past 14 years of my life crafting an intricate tale that evokes the mind and spirit. i am proud to bring you "Ghetto Sonic"

wint
@dril

136576751575904257

" GEnder?? i barely know her!
*cuts off dick&** "

what gender do i have to turn myself itno to be able to squirt octopus ink out

wint
@dril

165988799636193280

just doing some nude sunbathing in this gender neutral target restroom. i hope i dont get my dick sucked

wint
@dril

7326470680791326 72

genderman's only weakness is being told that his name contains a masculine bias

wint
@dril

88612912133976064

taco bell is all too eager to implement fourthmeal BUT has yet to acknowledge Fourthgender. the almighty dollar folks

wint
@dril

26467449844

"do turds carry gneder. are there male turds & female turds." good question, Walter_PSX. hte answer, however, is not so clear cut im afraid;

wint
@dril

298619038081355776

revealing the gender of my baby by eating a whole bunch of food dye and taking a huge pink shit in front of my relatives. ah!! its a girl !!

wint
@dril

8755507286847744704

"This Whole Thing Smacks Of Gender," i holler as i overturn my uncle's barbeque grill and turn the 4th of July into the 4th of Shit

wint
@dril

213849618415484929

please keep my denny's coupon gender rant off of wikipedia's list of notable tantrums-- it is NOT notable

wint
@dril

3171317205226225024

how d o i subtly let my hairdresser know that i want her to cut my dick off instead of my hair

wint
@dril

213843017751203842

# GAMESTOP

*"Girls are my wife constantly"*

#ImSingleBecause my grasp of humen sexuality far exceeds that of eveyr girl

wint
@dril

2141962178868075010

my romantic girl friend sees the super blood moon reflected in my greased back hair and pledges then and there to bow to christ our master

wint
@dril

648282094104379393

my promise to all women: my promise to all women is that i will seal theur nudes in a velvet envelope, and wont open it until im 100 yrs old

wint
@dril

8470467367778547200

every woman ivr ever spoken to would describe our correspondence as "Graceful"

wint
@dril

620647779271114752

local singles want to meet you in YOUR AREA! click here to call the COPS

wint
@dril

4051969492020101112

#ToTheGirls2016 im intelligent & clean boy. i have the trigger dicispline of a lion. ive used Torture to cure myself of all mental illness.

wint
@dril

690237259451387904

THinking of a "Boy's Day" of twitter..won't post specifics due to trolls, but basically all girls will nicely be asked to log out for 24hrs,

wint
@dril

619412570848391168

women aare setting unrealistic body standards by expecting me to wear a tuxedo 24/7 and to not flip out at waiters

wint
@dril

929782162337030144

going t o start saying, "Wife City" whenever i see an attractive woman. e.g... "thats Wife City" or "that girl is Wife City to me"

wint
@dril

828104135400706049

i want all every girl on twitter to take the pH level of here pussy and send it to me via private email

wint
@dril

14968219634769920

where do girls live

wint
@dril

27970378831

Jsut arranged an 8-count box of pop tarts to be sent to a girls house. Looking forward to explaining to her how to prepare them

wint
@dril

823786384020357121

group of young woman: were going to take some "Selfie" portraits. care to join us?
me [doing the face palm face now]:
ABSOLUTELY NOT!!!!!!!!

wint
@dril

428531292167475200

I shoudl not be expected to put my knee on the ground to propose to a woman, the same ground where the animals shit,

wint
@dril

673949340994531329

#ConfusingThingsGirlsDo show virtually no interest in The Bible Code

wint
@dril

142460383964303360

wint
@dril

(girl tells me shes sick) aahh that sucks so much. you can come over & have some of my mens one a day vitamins. probably works on girls too,

8407968541913088802

wint
@dril

#TagABeautifulGirl im good. im really good and normal. i want to take a women to the shooting range and discuss guns culture. i love humor

386656001471954945

wint
@dril

wasup babe., im a normal person. *walks on down to next girl* Wassup babe, im a normel person . *moseys over to another lady* wasup babe, im

1457591261117548033

wint
@dril

i hate i t when girls think im proposing whenever i take the knee at them in protest

930209246297448453

wint
@dril

im watching my gf transform into wolves . the wolves have the same tattoos that she have. she can turn back into a person when she wants to.

2823964066692601856

girls always love to telling people not to " Mansplain" but they do not care of, "Man's Pain"

wint
@dril

754537489805828096

i chew on my philly cheesesteak as i place a camera under the table to film womens' feet. Klout.com - The Standard for Influence.

wint
@dril

221452655304773632

obliviously driving m y car through chernobyl , absorbing lethal anmounts of radiation while looking for cute girls

wint
@dril

201923985007575040

paying women to ram me with thier cars

wint
@dril

854524960957747200

#Zodiacfacts #scorpio women have two ass holes

wint
@dril

11723543295

(intentionally spoken within earshot of severral arbys girls) ah fuck. my hands smell like steroids from using steroids all day

wint
@dril

6498595695905906028352

every one always says they would use x-ray goggles to look at womens asses and get horny and wild. Not me. I would use them to help doctors

wint
@dril

5680805571425026048

All girls have exactly $100,000

wint
@dril

9055202786612176898

i love to hover hand my gf in pictures. (gets Owned across various media) sorry. Sorry everyone. I forgot that was bad

wint
@dril

6191780625580617217

oh look–i failed my forklift operators certification for the 4th fucking time becausse none of the girls on here bothered fucking helping me

wint
@dril

1015343021313884160

*"god wil put me in his pocket"*

just inherited about 200 crude dog statues my grandma sculpted to scare Angels away from her propertyl,

wint
@dril

27645326518

indeed, god is starting another great flood but this time he wants the ark filled with a shitload of monster and red bull instead of animals

wint
@dril

223108477202075648

need some new Christian podcasts to listen to while cruising around in my fake cop car

wint
@dril

433661974820712448

you know society is ASS-FUCKED when people spend more time wiritng "Tweets", than bibles

wint
@dril

845450020170141697

i touch a glowing qur'an and turn into 100 lions #suitswag

wint
@dril

150679311756705792

i just hacked into the church and made god REal

wint
@dril

564508071779516416

what happens when kirby swallows the qur'an and is granted its considerable power. my 81 chapter fanfic explores this issue -- and more

wint
@dril

213844275102883840

you wanna come to my church & post about me sucking tiny ladybug dicks on the bulletin board? mm nope. that ain't me pal. That ain't my life

wint
@dril

392326968064360449

my big sons have made a mess of the garage again after being riled up by the good word of the Lord

wint
@dril

537598363534123008

how come a baby born with a foot in its brain is considered a "Miracle Baby" but when I get my dick stuck in a drawer im just some asshole

wint
@dril

176512142944636929

*slams king james holy bible shut on a piece of pepperoni with mayo and onions stickin out * And that is how u make a truth sandwich

wint
@dril

1152307658679992320

please dont make whimsy of the popes ass while I am on-feed. ive more inportant things to do than indulge myself in hearsay of the popes ass

wint
@dril

5662756632888688648

just as Christ washed the feet of his disciples , i proudly volunteer to allow my girl followers to use my shirt as a napkin,.

wint
@dril

7579118481548697620

the vatican should not be allowed to name any new saints until God sorts out my numerous issues with the citibank web portal

wint
@dril

9778601412814315520

went to sons baptism. i yeled "Not so fast Champ" and punched the priest & spalshed holy water around. i lost my child in the ensuing chaos

wint
@dril

21059836372

PRIEST: in the name of the father...
ME: Yes. Good          PRIEST: ...the son..
ME: Great. Go on. keep em comin
PRIEST: ..and the Holy Spirit
ME: No

wint
@dril

722586067275247618

ive narrowed it down to the church of scientology & the united states marines. whichever one allows me to jerk off more wins the tiebreaker

wint
@dril

494260940502990850

itoday i realized that Miracles, Guardian Angels, God, it all exists; when i put 1000 bees on my dick and every single one of them stung it

wint
@dril

222227481703350273

IF THE ZOO BANS ME FOR HOLLERING AT THE ANIMALS I WILL FACE GOD AND WALK BACKWARDS INTO HELL

wint
@dril

205052027259195393

westboro baptist church head to the forest to picket the site of a fallen tree

wint
@dril

21316285730

im gonna eat this whole sack of potatoes by my self #AntiLent

wint
@dril

9244635947

i imagine to the lice who live in my chest hair, my enormous, frowning head is God; their only beacon of hope, thats why i never wear shirts

wint
@dril

3045849399811115392

I already discovered the Higgs-Boson particle in the trash can, with the rest of the hokum . #CERN #God #GodReal #GodIsReal #GodsReal

wint
@dril

2203870270305111616

congrats all. thanks to your tireless efforts, and unrelenting, coordinated aggression, the cheese cake factory now serves, "The Eucharist"

wint
@dril

863950010924376064

if someone can get me the quran written in saddam hussein's blood i will use it to craft a Blade and i will let you touch the blade one time

wint
@dril

233367606940274688

at last., after years of legal b.s. i am finally required to be served up to 5 communion wafers at church because im a big fat hungry man

wint
@dril

219331180561039360

there are only like 4 girls on this entire site, and theyve all blocked me for saying that snow white and the seven dwarfs are muslim

wint
@dril

908731690679488513

every 100 years ,the world votes for a new Bible, to replace the old one. i honourably submit: The Joe Dirt Novel, writen by Spade, as bibl.

wint
@dril

230321846006992897

christ washed the feet of his disciples but not the ass. never the ass

wint
@dril

387558776984715264

for every year that He is not featured in Forbes Magazine as the worlds richest man... GOD will sink one of our battle ships

wint
@dril

759404675468754944

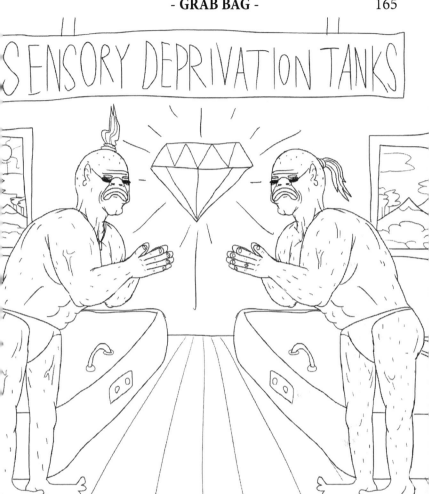

*two men emerge from sensory deprivation tanks*
*"I just attained oneness with all living beings"*
*"I just fucked the Girl rabbit from SpaceJam"*

delighting my friends and family by doing the chris rock routine about "The Big Piece of Chicken" but in a worse voice

wint
@dril

9233859050077734784

tried to overdose on aquarium pebbles & the hospital laughed at me and the ambulance drivers all took turns whipping me with catheter tubes

wint
@dril

185248218324537344

fifty two year old mamn hides underneath a tarp at work and jacks off to the same cartoon characters he did when he was thirty years younger

wint
@dril

521879274387931136

"Crowdpleasers"... Now these, I like

wint
@dril

622847048857968640

the desert has never helped any one and i am going to go throw poison at it

wint
@dril

396595443129282561

i dont know if i'm wearing it wrong or what but this Thick Load Bracelet is not making my loads thick.

wint
@dril

22096145660518400

jacking off is Alphamail

wint
@dril

842036465353781248

currently on a car ride with 8BitMarcus, who just tried to use the defroster to clean bird poop off of the window. what a dumb piece of shit

wint
@dril

1567314088818249728

*rotates earth 13 degrees* WHich zodiac sign are u now?? *rotates earth 27 degrees* NOW what one are u?? *rotates earth 2 degre* Fucker

wint
@dril

27130927146606592

looking for medicines that will make the fish in my koi pond shit less often

wint
@dril

955930287074172928

everytime jeff dunham makes his miserable puppets kiss each other a bridge collapses somewhere

wint
@dril

265482794371792896

do nOT buy "grab bag" option at the Onion Brothers' Onion Emporium. it is a trick devised to sell you undesirable onions

wint
@dril

326845025961013248

i gotta say it folks. breast milk tastes like SHIT., "Sorry ladies"

wint
@dril

1025030347707170817

girls legs 2017. legs getting shot by paintball guns. "Is legs normal." legs on the mind. annihilated by legs

wint
@dril

901873048390955009

my followers know im the go-to Bitch when it comes to interior wood paneling, so if i say its a "no buy", the shit has become seirious

wint
@dril

1011087835800141825

**wint**
**@dril**

(a) an alternate universe where im gay (b) an alternate universe where im bi (c) an alternate universe where alternate universes aren't real

233027919465824258

**wint**
**@dril**

\*stares at a man doing jumping jacks in complete awe\* How is he doing that

411115341163401216

**wint**
**@dril**

obliterating my load with a blow torch

922931912599130112

**wint**
**@dril**

sick of our media's unrealistic portrayal of Boomerangs , which are weak as shit in real life

508892439911096320

**wint**
**@dril**

top ten things you do NOT want to hear in the Nursing profession: 10. Shut the fuck up 9. Fuck you idiot 8. Your pay check is in the trash

913109321147437056

"*#GroundhogDay is the one day a year where the nation can put asaide the partisan politics and sacrifice a large rodent to God*"

wint
@dril

due to budget constraints the ground hog this year has been replaced by a caged man in a loincloth who also fears shadows

959389367470084096

 wint
@dril

lets see if that Awful Groundhog can predict six weeks of Electro House blaring directly into its shity cage

32821667843538944

 wint
@dril

i rip off my groundhog handler disguise on stage. "surprise bitchs. groundhog day is fake." i drop kick the fuckin groundhog back to the zoo

297866071157919745

 wint
@dril

groundhog sees a nude mans gyrating ass instead of shadow, predicting 6 weeks of erupting yellowstone supervolcano

170385313649278977

"*guns are the most inportant weapon of our time. lock and load. see you at the Range.*" - *anonymous*

461765121417940992

getting all the snow out of my driveway with a gun, just fucking obliterating it

wint
@dril

412315657640767489

gonna fill up on milk shakes and do some open carry off the grid

wint
@dril

714491528547143680

media outrage over the discovery of geiorge zimmerman's Gun Sink, a kitchen sink filled to the brim with guns

wint
@dril

405766223159242752

the sniper lifestyle requires perfect animal instincts and also smoking. dont join my sniper squad if u havent forsaken humanity& dont smoke

wint
@dril

377087244663672833

i am beginning to doubt that most of the subscribers to my feed are mature enough to handle sniper info.

wint
@dril

377091567359496193

Imagine. A world where guns come out of the ground like plants. And all the water is replaced by Bullet's. This is Gun World. It's real

wint
@dril

34912332027011072

Nobody Checks My Son For Head Lice With Out Getting Past My Police Issue Hollow Point Smith & Wesson Which Gives Everyone It Shoots Leukemia

wint
@dril

616378857462059008

when you do sutuff like... shoot my jaw clean off of my face with a sniper rifle, it mostly reflects poorly on your self

wint
@dril

7791618573577713409

jeopardy should give the contestants guns and make them shoot the categories. i think that this would improve the image of the guns brand

wint
@dril

537342974154534912

*wactches a sniper headshot a butterfly while its still inside of the cocoon* Hm, absolute Ownage. Ihave never seen anything that good.

wint
@dril

377076885286449152

cleanning my assault rifles with wads of toilet paper

wint
@dril

472157922240512001

the first rule about Guns is to Respect The Guns. NEVER let your dog lick the Guns. and don't point the Guns at anything unless it is bad

wint
@dril

228874030730575874

*ffires 400 rounds at a piece of shit log until it slumps over* Take that adam landza

wint
@dril

621299884923039745

i just want to find the optimal bra for sniper operations, but everoyne here is so rude, and pieces of shit

wint
@dril

677825110422790144

who will be brave enough to create a 3d motion picture about talking guns. who will let the guns tell their story

wint
@dril

383742058831179776

wint
@dril

this week's "Perfect Sniper Murder Hell Wish " goes out to that russian kid with cornrows who told me chester cheetah was a Dog in 5th grade

377074313779609600

wint
@dril

i show up at the range wearing a t-shirt that says "I Wont Wear The Earplugs" and i m promptly directed back to my car by staff members

621303063576358912

wint
@dril

jusut dropped 8000000 HKD on a usb-interfaced sniper rifle that blocks one of my insolent followers at random every time i pull the trigger

766474019436716032

wint
@dril

just sold 1000 guns to "CONGO" in my most radical act of self care to date

903040773985316864

wint
@dril

iwant to outfit the scope on my sniper rifle with net flicks

488183243901272064

getting shot directly in the ass execution style while crawling through a duct

wint
@dril

9499091341390825472

i feel like getting shot would;nt be that bad if you knew how to properly "body spin " away from the bullet or slap it away with your hand

wint
@dril

5519730626444883456

SOME ONE REPLACED MY INCEST FAQS WITH PICTURES OF TURKISH FLAGS AND GUNS

wint
@dril

1193984426681376769

a gun that is also a boomerang

wint
@dril

9087473459

attn: Fucker who posted False R.I.P. to Cedric The Entertainer; i haeve just received my good shooter degree from gun college. that is all

wint
@dril

473230045600093184

"*im sensing some major bullshit coming from the graveyard*"

there are rifts in the Frankenstein community regarding whether or not igor was tasked with jacking the monster off to keep it docile

wint
@dril

335432692931899392

im known to "Trick or Treat" from my neighbors mail boxes. they love it and it drives them wild. And it`s a bit of fun

wint
@dril

690522222172205056

can anyone confirm or deny that the "spooky dicks" they sell around halloween each year aren't just rebranded dildos

wint
@dril

390142331816386562

some say if you show your ass to the hell mirror you will feel the icy finger of the reaper touch the back of your bals

wint
@dril

218508899244982273

remember not to die on halloween so you dont turn into w pumpkin

wint
@dril

528077683146903552

pyramid was the first haunted hous.e Fact.

wint
@dril

2170872780136161 28

a nice tip for halloween: fill up a jar with piss and say that it is a jar of frankenstein piss. display it on the porch with a strobe light

wint
@dril

386992132579287040

"FEAR IS USED 2 ENSLAVE THE MASSES," I SAID AS I RIPPED THE FUCKIN DECORATIVE CARDBOARD SKELETON OFF OF THE COMMUNITY CENTERS BULLETIN BOARD

wint
@dril

2594125112149319 68

folks if you think haunted house is scary this halloween i invite you to look at the damn economy and thj dow jones

wint
@dril

915768434662748160

handing print outs of my most beloved arliss (arli$$) quotes to trick or treaters

wint
@dril

7932910991 50376964

"*my christ. i am invigorated. using my new official old spice dr.pepper halo 3 exfoliating forehead wax. this is God. this feeling is God*"

**wint**
**@dril**

threres a rumor master chief will take off his mask and reveal hes the btk killer.. do not do this.. it would be disrespectful to halo

539653749003022336

**wint**
**@dril**

congress members fighting over who can scream "halo 5" the loudest, until a senior member stands up and yells "halo 6", infuriating them all

15269318182

**wint**
**@dril**

yo this server is for pregnant halo players only. all u non pregs can go suck a lemon, capiche??

1982653766612687872

**wint**
**@dril**

fellas..tell your girls you will n ot be providing any more sex until the entire female race apologizes for halo 5's dismal metacritic score

663335941210292224

**wint**
**@dril**

#worstfeeling dying of dehydration caused by diarrhea in a third world nation ravaged by warfare with no doctors #bestfeeling halo 4 odst

5601478582

wint
@dril

"the definition of shuriken is extremely broad & encompasses any thrown weapon. a chair can be shuriken, for instance. a birdbath"-UncleHalo

503898677547909120

"*its fucked up how there are like 1000 christmas songs but only 1 song aboutr the boys being back in town*"

im not saying i dont respect the flag. just saying id respect it more if it was a picture of something thats good to me. like someones lunch

wint @dril

917488695393079296

please check out my devastating one-man takedown of the thanksgiving day parade, which was given a PG rating by the MPAA due to " sarcasm".

wint @dril

766462908222038017

once again, dick clark's diaper drops miserably around his ankles precisely at the stroke of midnight, signifying a grim year to come #2012

wint @dril

153353585223143424

my friend nasdaq_oscar says they just let all the pardoned turkeys run around the white house and shit on the carpet. disgrace to the office

wint @dril

537660379825192960

awfully bold of you to fly the Good Year blimp on a year that has been extremely bad thus far

wint @dril

490366979749216256

**wint**
**@dril**

my 2015 new years resolutions is to go to hell less often, and raise $99 by selling stolen mulch to buy my account back from lockheed martin

550398038314086400

**wint**
**@dril**

oh? you want me to take the bad santa posters off my car windows? sorry, i forgot that its a fucking fedearal crime to think things are good

1000270193875210240

**wint**
**@dril**

my uncles caught me searching "can i still join isis if im racist" on the family computer & are now withholding all holiday treats for 2015.

670194348017848320

**wint**
**@dril**

the mall santas all shit into a salad bowl hidden beneath their throne and the elves have to go wash it out in the fountain every hour or so

940983362860277761

**wint**
**@dril**

cant wiat to see what devilish thanksgiving scenarios me and the boys of twitter can conjure up. "The turkey was taken by spiders? ? Whua??"

536888193661304832

can;t believe people still try to rile me up in the year 2010

wint
@dril

7636381490

xmas hual 2011: can of paste, novel based on "little fockers", Oprah Crystals, fucken mmeat ball sandwich, a fuckin $2.50 slice-a pound cake

wint
@dril

151356070630141952

reminder that if you jerk off tomorrow on christmas y ou are the bastard of earth.

wint
@dril

283315931197894656

the latest rumor ;which i dont even care to discuss or give a shit about, is that i was seen drinking out of a bird bath on easter sunday

wint
@dril

465540544262066176

my favorite holiday is the one where you cover everything in plastic and turn the hose on indoors and just go wild

wint
@dril

439195904755511296

*"how did they do the ace ventura butt talk. i know that shit wasnt real. was it 3d or robots"*

"stuart little 2" isn;t funny. somebody had to say it

381462717371932672

Jacking off is a fool 's errand. I will instead opt to enjoy the films of Ice Age, Ice Age: The Meltdown and Ice Age: Dawn of the Dinosaurs.

435376359498448896

i can confirm that Somali pirates have intercepted my shipment of 20,000 glossy 8x10 headshots and are using them for vile purposes

362230103750606851

"tarzan of the apes" will never become a Turner Classic Movie. shoddy premise. people find pictures of a man yelling in the woods disgusting

710369819485446144

most important art movements in human history?? three way tie between impressionism, cubism, and Bullet Time

391413538595422208

wint
@dril

thinking about a adults version of star wars where all the characters have Depression and saying the word "Bauzinga" to mysef in my car

985512751685619712

wint
@dril

if youre looking for good movies about grease, do not watch the nmovie "grease", because you will get swindled

565081676124942339

wint
@dril

JAY: They are going to replace WTC, with a Mosque. Can you believe this Silent Bob SILENT BOB: This country is headed fot the chamber pot.

424183163175567360

wint
@dril

what i sent you just now was not my sizzle reel. it was a teaser for my sizzle reel., and if you were in the industry youd fucking know that

246949616350814208

wint
@dril

(genuflects as two golden lights come forth from behind me, taking the form of majestic angel wings) i would never hold a seleb at gun point

783011977580974080

**wint**
**@dril**

it is with a heavy heart that i must announce that the celebs are at it again

514845232509501440

**wint**
**@dril**

I have just obtained a historic deleted segment from Disney's Fantasia. It features a middle-aged man in an NFL jersey buying light bulbs

338223358153981952

**wint**
**@dril**

in my version of indiana jones he shoots the boulder with a sniper rifle hundreds of times instead of running away from it

464657630695542784

**wint**
**@dril**

oscars for exrtraordinarily subversive, insightful, online textual Musings?? unsoiled by MOneymen?? Thats what my shit particularly would be

569742496462450688

**wint**
**@dril**

i just got an email asking me to join The Rat Pack. need to know if its real or not before i move to belarus to make textiles with my uncles

369452664444026880

**wint**
**@dril**

My Regular Life And My Ocean's Eleven Fanfiction Life Have Collided In A Horrible Fire Ball

9800502979

**wint**
**@dril**

AVATAR didnt win enough oscars, please supporrt independent film maker james cameron b y cutting your oscar statue in half (if you have one)

10219988211

**wint**
**@dril**

yo hollywood! check THIS out! *flops over face forward, lies still, becomes dust over the course of 100 years and is separated by the wind*

22321405438

**wint**
**@dril**

if someone wins an oscar and they start crying they should rip it out of the Fucker's hands #Oscars

1739663717795902464

**wint**
**@dril**

vin diesel as the Tooth Fairy??? Now I've seen every thing.

7718528986

**wint**
**@dril**

movies that portray Dragons in a positive light are marked with a gold marble, while movies racist against Dragons are given a frowning Ass.

152425474214211586

**wint**
**@dril**

has any one ever noticed that the good spiderman movies are the ones for adults, and the bad spiderman movies are the ones for children

692694457074991105

**wint**
**@dril**

stood up, faced audience during larry the cable guy movie, and shouted "YOu're all monsters, stop laughing at him, that's his regular voice"

409256729260482560

**wint**
**@dril**

i dedicate this oscar to the caveman who invented electricity, because without him— Film would cease

364328659470921729

**wint**
**@dril**

some hipster or something is probably mad right now bc they give golden globes to good ass films instead of the fuckin mona lisa or whatever

422551984177033216

chaplain era silent motion pictures where basically the first subbed anime . click to read more

wint
@dril

590498719562407937

i just bought an Oscar on the black market and im willing to give it to the first bbw to send me a pic of herself fisting ehr own mouth.

wint
@dril

309030815453560832

with advancements in technology we will someday be able to watch a 3d animated version of larry the cable boy go to vegas & get into trouble

wint
@dril

350933791205900288

i love "Going hollywood" by retweeting burger king and lock heed martin 1000 times

wint
@dril

916874280528502784

the boys held an intervention about me "Going hollywood" because i;ve been buying plastic toothpicks now

wint
@dril

1002620684286287872

"*I'm Sgt. General James Bond. My mission is to collect guns and gather intel on the unimaginably fucked up drugs known as Cocaine & Marijuana*"

4098591753724518840

woah . the movie theaters are handing out pendants which glow whenever James BOnd gets laid during the movie #Good #ImmersionTech

wint
@dril

152425474214211586

ENJOYING BOND MMO?? JUST CRAFTED SOME REMARKABLE BOND GEAR WHILE YOU WERE BUSY TRYING TO FUCK THE NPCS WITH THE HUNDREDS OF OTHER JAME BONDS

wint
@dril

593477944061853698

james bonds jet black diapers that cost $200 each. suit jacket that has Jame bonds signature drawn on the pocket. james bond engagement ring

wint
@dril

998634912981966848

james bond learns how to do cartwheels from a wise eskimo on top of mt. everest and uses them to roll through a nuclear blast unscathed

wint
@dril

596349448432787457

(saying loud enough so people can hear) the matrix is the james bond of steam punk

wint
@dril

667317443719659520

wint @dril
the man who froze his shit and cut them into tiny disks to fool the coinstar machine is probably the closest thing to real life james bone .

2942269095822204928

 wint @dril
i squat down, leaving a tiny, perfect marble of shit in the lobby of four seasons hotel in honolulu. i then contact my associate, James Bond

234168900005294080

 wint @dril
bond theme plays while super spy & ladys man James Bond wanders around the forest with a magnifying glass, searching for the cure for autism

1194054354220803072

 wint @dril
james bond, your next assignment is to infiltrate the white house and take the Tax's back from obama. please, get the Tax's -

26912661658

 wint @dril
JAMES BOND: (Shoots his gun at the screen in the intro and murders me) ME: Now that;s cinema

5236259398851563009

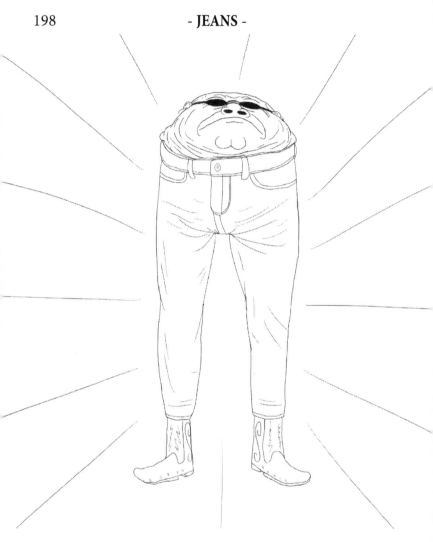

"*the fact is, my children are going to see people wearing Jeans on television, in the movies, and other media. how do i explain that to them*"

wint
@dril

alrigth who shoved a pair of jeans into the chilean miners' airhole and got it stuck. that was a lousy gift

26976284807

wint
@dril

i had my jeans bronzed as an infant. and they still fit mother fucker

4919326354179563355

wint
@dril

im a fruad. i wear the wrangler jeans despite never having wrangled a single goddamn thing in my life

513390599135694848

wint
@dril

my combat jeans deflect most bow and arrows shots and also prevent me from thinking about sex

478457030106427392

wint
@dril

did i jsut piss myself? no . these are mood jeans that change color when i am sick of putting up with jokers such as your self

216930169028476928

wint
@dril

a mudslide engulfs a small village as I obliviously powerwash my bluejeans uphill

3533115732148879379

wint
@dril

i will admit that sometimes i crash my car on purpose just so i can get a faceful of my Denim Airbags

221035915529814021

wint
@dril

my résumé; page 1 ; "IM A JEANS MAN FIRST AND FOREMOST" in 42pt. rosewood font. page 2 is the bible

401014348758384464

wint
@dril

installed 28 Mods on this pair alone. wrangler, levi.. they all want me dead,m because i refuse to offer them my talents. the jeans hacker .

231690600615919616

wint
@dril

although im the foremost Blue Jeans Virtuoso i consider it disrespectful to wear them. i simply kiss each pair 5 times a day; facing mecca.

167655059570696194

wint
@dril

a small, ramshackle town where nearly every adult male has a severe case of blue lung from being forced to work in the denim mines

2427214905361112128

wint
@dril

blue jean's... Activated .

7955603160799313393

wint
@dril

fucking CHRISt. this dipshit clerk at hollister has been rtrying to run my denim credit card thru the reader for like 10 mins. go to College

2193295946311782400

wint
@dril

im just a Hispanic male who loves looking at pictures of bluejeans. i have a tough road ahead and a long ways 2 go in my life

13349849255

wint
@dril

THE COP GROWLS "TAKE OFF TH OSE JEANS, CITIZEN." I COMPLY, REVEALING THE FULL LENGTH DENIM TATTOOS ON BOTH LEGS. THE COP SCREAMS; DEFEATED

1909430807304722448

*"if you don't know how to use a Lathe you deserve to eat dog shit"*

remember to always have samples of urine, shit, semen and blood attached to your belt to avoid wasting the doctor';s time if you get sick

517598959578406912

im delighted to see that people are waking up to the fact that Masturbation is fraud, and turns all of the T in your body into germs

550809014016409600

as far as im concerned the best revenge is ordering wolf piss online & pouring it into soneones car. "living well" is too hard

wint
@dril

390487678715957249

eating baby food. baby food for adults. adult baby food. i eat baby food. eat baby food as an adult. tricks to eating baby food as an adult.

wint
@dril

31408907805003776

calmly browisng my 100 Sites per day, as recommended by the experts

wint
@dril

854070752223649792

109 year old man attributes long life to uncircumcised dick, no vaccines,

578842648989011968

***pisses all over shower faucets, wife's luffa, candles, knocks shampoo bottles off shelf with piss stream** it's fine because its sterile

wint
@dril

397755117690032129

the secret fruit that oprah eat`s to become more psychic can now be ordered "ONLINE"

wint
@dril

563608431483813890

this is the national health advisory board issuing a safe reminder not to touch your dick for one hour after handling pets

wint
@dril

399002223599841280

if i learned anything in business school its that you can disarm any competitor by insinuating he carries his turds around in his briefcase

wint
@dril

390183972946595840

i burned 100 extra calories today just by thinking aobut asses

wint
@dril

502323328397606912

you gotta cut the shrimp down the middle to get that good turd out,

wint
@dril

479268156226011136

doctor: i can say with absolute certainty that if you do one more weird trick youll die
me: CAPTAIN TIGER's Miracle Corn. LOok it up bastard

wint
@dril

567333455353360385

doing head stands to let the cum from my balls flow directly to my brain and make me more intelligent

wint
@dril

971787472257548288

geting a bunch of reptile habitat sun lamps to beam some much needed vitamin d into my fucking obese skull while i do the rounds on sites

wint
@dril

912568949132361728

just tape the car horn down and cars will naturally move away from you. you can drive anywhere. it is called, "The Instinct of the Beast"

wint
@dril

4069168407454842288

YOU WILL NEVER WASH YOURSELF AGAIN AFTER WATCHING THIS WISE OLD YOUTUBE CLIP WHICH HAS BEEN BANNED BY DOCTORS

wint
@dril

479268156226011136

every room in every home must have a Host

wint
@dril

619297689478389760

adding "A Touch of Class" to my home by wrapping all of my game's apparatuse's in tinsel

wint
@dril

664809067051941890

spice up your life by throwing your favorite coffee mug into the garbage

wint
@dril

664809705232080896

wint
@dril

baths and showers are fucking stupid; here's what u do: get one of those big rotisserie ovens and roatate inside of it until you're dead

1417340444288808193

wint
@dril

vineger contains so much energy.. thats why moms call it, "Free Money"

7797457239821 80352

wint
@dril

today. i will stay home and sharpen my balls. i will Hone My Balls

268030382904061954

wint
@dril

i feel like if i practiced often enough and really focused i could learn how to shave all the hair off of my body using only my fingernails

284920854402453504

wint
@dril

never allow yourself to be loved. treat the Burger King brand with respect. celebrate ramadan EVERY month. end moms. vote with ur skateboard

2305343122 13241856

**wint**
**@dril**

i pay a man $3000.00 a month to stream line my feed so i can get more jokes per second about putin saying "hold my beer" or what have you

957345115227545601

**wint**
**@dril**

football?? Pfuh. while you sweathogs are pounding off to grievous injury porn i'll be experiencing life at the car wash, with shorter lines

5620264469380358144

"*Flying to Dubai, UAE, to jack off in a hotel room.*"

were you surprised to see me, gaming in the bathtub?? i am a man of infinite pleasure. come, hand me my robe. i write my own mr. bean skits

wint
@dril

387066929816420352

im a pleased as punch spoon-fed bitch and thats a bottom line

wint
@dril

5774851380298629l3

i feell like im being unfairly targeted during this paintball match just because im the only one wearing a tuxedo

wint
@dril

4365700651323228l7

pissed off by my nintendo peripherals and other stupid shit rattling around toomuch in my $1600 brief case

wint
@dril

8838318046036418s6

need to wash gamefuel stains out of a very expensive kimono

wint
@dril

4071833347672023o4

Eatinh a 26 dollar hoagie.

wint
@dril

5705902565059870

mean while, while you were "Gaming ", i
tasted 100 different wines in a cave behind a
waterfall and cried into a shaman's arms

wint
@dril

378130907804098560

installing a cyborg tube in my tuxedo which
frequently sprays my ass with various
advanced powders

wint
@dril

9089931333387579393

my mansion sucks

wint
@dril

4663846463188882816

huge disgusting man with extremely
muscular fingers pokes at his tiny laptop
while his emaciated servants groom him
with squeegees #win

wint
@dril

3784384078708776966

"*people please, all i ask for is one town hall meeting which doesnt reference The Matrix*"

measure to approve massive depressing statue in the center of town depicting an emaciated mayor carrying a boulder that says "My Sons" on it

5154710555587405824

angel-voiced 5'2" man forbidden by mayor from performing at this years christmas pageant— "described as upsetting" "this tradition must end"

7737948889928333824

middle-aged men have been retreating to the sewers of our fair city to cry. as mayor i will promise to eradicate these terrible crying men

2062269852681558464

the mayor has erected another insulting effigy of me (myself) foir the local children to hurl stones and urine upon. lost my vote bitch

11216892362

i will respect the wishes of th e mayor and the townsfolk by not fucking the pumpkin patch and ruining the harvest, only if i am given $100.

7620134666534223872

Im at town hall getting a permit to have
e xtremely bad opinions about guitars

wint
@dril

519076254595969024

im sorry every one. the mayor ran out of key
to the cities so they had to give me the key
to all the girls bathrooms instead

wint
@dril

895535292437811200

"spend a lot of time thinking about how sometimes even war criminals can be heroes sometimes... Dont like it? Click the unfollow buttobn"

Hell Yes;. the army is putting me and my guns on a plane back to iraq. Thius is like real life DLC

wint
@dril

489071962174414848

us military displays extremely rare princeess diana beanie baby w/ certificate of authenticity in the most devastating show of force to date

wint
@dril

911698994363092993

im rwriting a script about a smart and handsome army man cop who murders civilians but wants to stop murdering civilians because hes in love

wint
@dril

5184082093389072384

the scud missile was named after famous military physicist Scud Missile

wint
@dril

408466746861826048

watch this marines Epioc response to being told that he should replace his gun with an enormous lollipop

wint
@dril

885886605206183937

please let me cover my entire webpage in jungle camo so soldiers can research vital murder info on the battlefield without being spotted

wint
@dril

638724393506578432

i think if we lower the legal army age to maybe llike, 12, we will see a sharp decrease in recreational nudity

wint
@dril

511808294785388544

the conflicted supersoldier stares over the horizon as he smokes a cigarette. "war is the most fucked up thing ever." he takes a sip of beer

wint
@dril

381535376755531776

us military strikes deal with PepsiCo to waterboard all terror suspects with Mt Dew??? wish i had some of that Free Dew. who is john galt

wint
@dril

1862906450812928

nuke obtained by renegade AssFreak

wint
@dril

559101688788058113

Give this the retweet if you agree that ALL beanie babies deserve to be worth $100 , and also that Water boarding is not tortore

wint
@dril

940396058546491392

baffled as to why the powers that be would insist that me, my Hotwif,e & paramour Hubby can not enlist in the marines together as a Squadron

wint
@dril

1028753069058613248

border colies are 250% Smarter than humans and stronger to, which is why the US Military refuses to breed them

wint
@dril

53432941338042368

all dressed up in my little tuxedo and ready to sacrifcie my self to isis

wint
@dril

524534181632942080

learning how to say "1 2 3" and "hut hut hut" at army

wint
@dril

909174040891359234

I own the best law firm in the tri-state area, my wife earns $200,000 a year making ginger bread houses, and we will never hire a US Veteran

wint
@dril

953621866178138112

a cool prank is to convince someone to join the Armed Forces and watch them get spooked by guns & missiles in exchange for hollow gratitude

wint
@dril

379549752590741505

the soldiers crafted armor out of the covers of outdated guinness world record books, to bedazzle and confound their opponents

wint
@dril

146391698078048257

just the other day i was taking a bath and i saw a tiny tugboat in there leaving a chemtrail. i told it to fuck off. im a green beret gunman

wint
@dril

475489616016195584

just thought off an idea i believe to be bad ass. lets find the address of the leader of isis, and mail him/ her pieces of our SHIT

wint
@dril

749048949642846208

the unsung heroes of the front lines, the diaper medics who face certain death to change our troops and wipe their asses during heavy combat

wint
@dril

225976127334797312

ARMY: your nickname reflects poorly on us all. we're changing it to something like "raven" or "switchknife"
ME: no. "hostage killer" is good

wint
@dril

5930174711172382720

im joining the army and then im joining ufc if im not too fucked up from the army. and thats the cold facts

wint
@dril

473717866303217665

i put years of hard work into getting my torture degree at torture college & now everyones like "oh tortures bad",",its ineffective" fuck off

wint
@dril

544197494755037185

phew. just served 4 years in afghanistan and not a single person saw my dick while I was over there. not one. hope they got a medal for that

wint
@dril

338383792744050689

"me and my friend bill gates live in fort knox now and if theres one thing i enjoy laughing all the way to its the bank"

wint
@dril

CLERK: Do you have your reward card
ME: Absolutely I do not. I shan't be taking
money out of the hands of Best Buy using
insidious exploits.

580628154856931328

wint
@dril

some people sing the praises of the one
hundred dollar bill... i myself, prefer the
humble, time-tested and reliable one dollar
bill

661837735729172480

wint
@dril

if i had a billion dollars id get wall-to-wall
carpeting in my bathroom and donate the
rest of it to the army

502855835832557569

wint
@dril

i dont trust banks. especially the pig shaped
ones

462232916815118336

wint
@dril

my stystem can predict all lottery numbers
with 100% accuracy. but not the powerball
number. it is too powerful

900594019453075456

there is NOTHING wrong with having 1 Million Doallrs

you are NOT defined by your one million dollars...

having 1 Million Dollars is normal

wint
@dril

7912263889970087232

list of casinos I need to burn down in order to prevent my credit score from going to the dogs: ceaser palace, trump cube, chuck e cheese,

wint
@dril

3897680385557294592

getting my loan approved at the bank by lying on my back and executing a series of flawless air kicks right there in the lobbby

wint
@dril

3300078760374263808

the first step to becoming a Millionaire is to acquire one hundred dollars

wint
@dril

7019152538865639936

pass the savings onto me mother fucker

wint
@dril

5645272300068334593

shiting into a tube while earning $4 an hour from home

wint
@dril

855438637726617600

wow this 40lb bag of dog food is only $30... why do dogs get all the bargains

wint
@dril

622121283371663360

farm boss: yyoure so good at cleaning the pigs' ass holes. please let us pay you
me: no. i won't allow my work to be corrupted by the dolar.

wint
@dril

5267300836600703488

that guy who makes all the ffuuu comics must have a milion dollars by now, mean while i live in a gutted bureau

wint
@dril

29691290954240002

waking up in a cold sweat and screaming about needing one million dollars, the amount of money made famous by Dr. Evil in austin powers 1 .

wint
@dril

987599876774088704

wint
@dril

i sit down at my cubicle, roll up m y pants and pick scabs off of my legs for 9 hours, ignoring evoery call & email i receive. i make $76/hr

2521608955543183336

wint
@dril

if they decide to replace the failing US dollar with killer quotes and refs from pg13 comedies then me and a lot of cool people will be rich

3796066818160271366

wint
@dril

the $100000 pyramid is actually fairly fucking cheap for a pyramid

7167320324963041286

wint
@dril

LIKE WANTING TO KNOW WHEN I GET TO SAVE BIG BUCKS FOR PENNYS ON THE DOLLAR AND GET RICH CHEAP

6677635734945218576

wint
@dril

I lvoe giving thousands of dollars to my real friends while kicking my fake friends asses

8762959015554129926

"i love doing the shitty pushups where my knees are touching the ground and counting them as real pushups"

eating 1/2 lb of beef boulougnase and getting roid rage from it

806055758773309440

i finally worked up enough courage to cry in front of the pregnant woman who frequents my gym

375381141483556864

these flawless squats on the roof of my van go out to the bastard who accused me of "going apeshit" a t wild birds unlimited in marietta, ga

314604834391216129

i just obtained a tub of that goop they fed to babies in the 1920s to make them really fat. i;m going to convert the whole thing into muscle

420907771211427840

gonna print out a bunch of pages from rival muscle blogs and scatter them across my driveway & drive my noisy scooter around on top of them

181206657051803648

my gym teacher is outside my house right now screaming about how I owe him 20 pushups from 1973 and that my torso sucks

wint
@dril

328866055307018242

the ONLY way to gain musclemass is to eat tiny lady bugs

wint
@dril

25557200987

(vomits while dioing pushups at the gym and resists every attempt from professional trainers to stop me from continuing)

wint
@dril

6372623757729672192

that three stooge thing where you run around in circles on the floor horizontally is actually a vital component of my yakuza training

wint
@dril

5245376177711640577

getting too big from steroids and smoking cigaretts in front of girls, walking around like a dumb ass, waddling like i got a log in my pants

wint
@dril

883829285269770240

glued a bunch of steaks to my body & did some poses & got the 2012 olympic muscle man medal & threw it in the trash cause its commercialized

wint
@dril

2303111184795054080

injecvting a shit ton of steroids and walking on the treadmill at 3mph

wint
@dril

996099712020336641

these are the same steroids that cops use... and you can now order them online for the very first time

wint
@dril

7788548139991829504

CALLING ALL MUSCLEFREAX— a country named "Ethiopia"' severely lacks Muscles. let's hit the bench and get heavy in their honor. #MuscleCrisis

wint
@dril

359461205930291200

looking to "Max Out" my ball's

wint
@dril

901122853260730368

workin out in a graduated cylinder. as i gain muscle mass the water level will rise above my head and drown me. this is true muscle suicide

wint
@dril

189363913966628865

do not ever come to my gym with crayons and draw smiley faces all over the walls. i will put your ass in the gutter. i will knock you over

wint
@dril

996465711533973504

muscle economy, muscles as currency, end the dollar, get ripped, get rich pumping weights, weatlh = body size, predicted by Blaise Pascal

wint
@dril

132123696079962113

i must rotate in my seat eternally to avoid having my muscles damaged by wi-fi energy

wint
@dril

427988439179333632

a 38 year old man who is dressed like a school shooter is here too pick up his vitality supplements .

wint
@dril

524924484911124481

eovery single day i thank God for my perfect skin and soft kissable lips as i wrap barbed wire around my arms and legs

wint
@dril

2188729057470013632

put pictures of fat 1920s babies up next to the muscle builders of modern day & you will ssee that their skill levels are considerably equal

wint
@dril

420909397548621824

think you got it rough? try engineering blog posts while trying to suck down two whole baby bottles full of muscle milk before Solstice ends

wint
@dril

3398693851728556832

"EGYPTIAN PROTESTERS
AIRDROPPED 100000 COPIES OF
"NOW THATS WHAT I CALL MUSIC
VOLUME 7"... THE SINGLE GREATEST
NTWICM ALBUM OF ALL TIME"

31413389045538816

**wint**
**@dril**

if you like the band sex pistols you will also enjoy my band called "the gun pistols"

4779138197136384400

**wint**
**@dril**

no you listen to me, Fucker, i need "Steppenwolf" carved into THE BLADE, not the handle-- please hold my father is crying

30311579119525888

**wint**
**@dril**

the dj who makes crude dog noises on my radio every day should listen to my rare metals podcast & learn how a real content producer behaves.

3494972723897330305

**wint**
**@dril**

U have to listen to this song "Signs" by the five man electrical band... the guy is just owning the fuck out of all these signs, it's insane

689575028820709376

**wint**
**@dril**

[[[[[[[[[[[[[[[[[[[[[[[[[[[[[please let Miley join the USMC]]]]]]]]]]]]]]]]]]]]]]]]]]]]] [[[[[[[[[[[[[[[[She will do good]]]]]]]]]]]]]]]]

541391199941443585

wint
@dril

" If U like a good song
I wont steer ya wrong
Cocaine
Its Got guitar and drums
So please listen to some
Cocaine "

615640902736969728

wint
@dril

indie punk rock band "THe 9/11 Forgetters"
wanted by police after imploring their
audience NOT to watch ABC's wednesday
night comedy lineup

320719903269212160

wint
@dril

downloading some very interesting pictures
of DJs

874893835213688836

wint
@dril

i am a Doctor and a Lawyer who will teach
u how to seduce women with rap music. my
name... is not important.

119036093860411344

wint
@dril

missin the glory days of the 90s when
true talent like "justin bieber" made
trending topic isntead of nonsense such as
"Beckhams face"

16028685743

wint @dril

i plan on attending chad and avril's wedding so i can absorb all the Love and Music Energy and use it to repair the corrupted soul of gaia .

238258215358435328

 wint @dril

Welcome to the citadel of eternal wisdom. Behold, this crystal contains the sum of all human knowledge -- Except Rap And Country

26334898832

 wint @dril

just had a nightmare that my account was permanently suspended for referring to "the beach boys" as "the beach boy shit boys"

917376225244573696

 wint @dril

meat loaf just ordered the venue to keep the lights on the audience so he can see if any trolls have infiltrated his show

782462016283938816

 wint @dril

my favorite part of the classic 16 tons song is when he threatens to kill me and beat the shit out of me for no reason in the middle of it

858360521078210560

wint
@dril

"When the moon hits your eye like a big pizza pie that's amore" nope. not true "When the world seems to shine like you'v" thats bullshit too

388524854300774400

wint
@dril

Electric Light Orchestra AND Spyro The Dragon??? Finally , A KickStarter I Can Empty My 401k Into

127149167750557696

wint
@dril

on a rickety stage at some empty roadhouse, a True mississippi blues man is howling aobut diapers, unappreciated by the toilet using masses

3147803186976563320

wint
@dril

like this if youre one of the 3% of teens who remembers when music was just guys saying "my name is kid rock" over and over

562785655680667648

wint
@dril

having a cocaine.mid ringtone does not make me a bad father.

26775833142

"every morning i pick up the local paper and read the latest condemnations about my rinky-dink, slipshod Ass & my child-like shoulder blades"

keurig is building a Mausque inside of a Dave and Busters, and Heres why it matters:

wint
@dril

930478104350478336

50 Year Old Man Tracks Down 12 Year Old Cyberbully And Kills Him With Whip "... And That's The Last Neopets Funeral U Will Ever Interrupt"

wint
@dril

23522764811927552

i got in the newspaper twice. once for my good posts, and once for screaming while still in the womb somehow

wint
@dril

602861798354755585

CNN NEWSWIRE: the guy who voiced the dog in the beggin strips commercials is now "beggin;" the american public to put a stop to jade helm 15

wint
@dril

862852259918512128

handsome single adutl man contracts scurvy after eating nothing but oscar mayer lunchables for 4 years and blames his dentist

wint
@dril

453367965283799040

hello newsweek? yeah im not gonna make it for that interview. some schmuck just pissed all over me. im covered head to toe in schmuck piss.

wint
@dril

394356502107914240

the News; - death cured; immortality real -on-line ghoul given plaque; recognized as "loudest human alive" - bird infiltrates macaroni grill

wint
@dril

558421033284538368

muting people who like to talk aobut "The news" instead of posting vignettes about being forced to pour mouthwash down their ass crack

wint
@dril

925741283456487424

You Won't Believe How Many Legs That Spiders Have

wint
@dril

521885937274720256

hgeuhkl i am a 300-pound producer / jurnalist my hobbies include car & beard maintenance also i know photoshop and my name is Miami

wint
@dril

29501331799

journalism is the hardest job on earth...I have to look at so many sites, and everyones trying to trick me into posting pics of my whole ass

wint
@dril

949473097459085313

(sees a cop shoot somone) This is just like james bond (sees a war happen) This is like robo cop (sees a burning house) This is like top gun

wint
@dril

754131489516818432

police are finding lots of Bad Food, theyve been yanking it otu of the ocean for about 10 minutes now on the news, i pray for the families

wint
@dril

2535545687

Disgusting Pear Man Fucks His Hideous Orange Wife -- Read More: Reuters.com

wint
@dril

20500500147343360

(wearing one of those fucking stupid hats with the word "Press" on it) mr president! do you think DC Films should show bat man taking a shit

wint
@dril

786511276113432577

wint
@dril

- Incest Prank Goes Wrong - Why Thousands Of Geniuses Are Ditching Their Aquariums - Can Plants Make You Smarter? - Moms Can Get Tattoos Now

756643017830834176

wint
@dril

i highly suggest using hash tag #HuckleGate if you're a Journo who wants to print my tougjh but fair opinions regarding huckle berry hound

575649523499954176

wint
@dril

BREATHTAKING: clever husband sells all of his sons war medals on ebay as punishment for exceeding family plan data caps

790081849490046976

"CAN GOD RESPECT GROUND ZERO SO MUCH THAT EVEN HE CANNOT BUILD A MOSQUE ON IT"

Sept 11: it is a testament to the resolve of our nation that the nine one one towers are still standidng upright and intact to this very day

wint
@dril

3922021582

[man leans into doorway of WTC bathroom] "Hey, you gotta finish up in there. 9/11 is happening." "Alright. Just a sec."

wint
@dril

4576756446970634240

judge dredd kicks the doors of the wtc mosque wide open and says "Well this looks like a big bunch of crap to me "

wint
@dril

5753048206571028488

i got banned from the official red lobster forums for posting "9/11". yet they say we're living in a post-9/11 world.....

wint
@dril

4100986644519237632

thanks for banning mme for having the username "WTCPuncher" , even though I registered that name before hte towers blew up in a car accident

wint
@dril

2973821132531589123

wint
@dril

hell of a week folks. first the apple press conference fails to impress me and now it's 9/11. whats next

510213279885828096

wint
@dril

proposed "slime wtc" catches airplanes and converst them into waste

181212052235362304

wint
@dril

my velcro jeans burst open, scattering my secret stash of 2 liter canada dry bottles as I stumble backwards off the roof of the 9/11 buildig

2027855052790094784

*"thinking about shit that i Recognize and smiling"*

**wint**
**@dril**

all the wonderful fictional characters i remember from my suburban middle-class 90s childhood break into my home & scrutinize my filthy dick

3006969124310042560

**wint**
**@dril**

while you were watching the teen choice awards, i was watching the classic episodes of the teen choice awards from back when they were good.

6864158861190776320

**wint**
**@dril**

proud to announce that after 30 years as a slave on my uncle's fishing vessel i no longer wish to fuck the post cereals honey-comb wanter

528305819600060417

**wint**
**@dril**

the good things i like about 90s is there were no hipsters, no rap, and your odds of getting an infection at a hospital were slightly higher

329229743083880449

**wint**
**@dril**

found in 100 yr time capsule: will o the wisp, a screaming bible, a fistful of shitty paper, some teeth, grandpas pipe, misc turds and husks

239223578191593472

best 90s memory is gathering around the old oak tree with the boys and passing around trading cards featuring all of our dads #DamnGood90s

wint
@dril

329220520434364416

#why90srocked everyothing was more real. everythig more visceral. a more 'human' experience. i was also 200 pounds less fat

wint
@dril

9940031934308353

i wish i had my baby teeth back. those were the good 90s teeth

wint
@dril

526101702186139648

"ive decided that nudity is acceptable if irt's done for artistic reasons, like, promoting a mattress store,"

fat nude man in guy fawkes mask sucked up by jet engine while doing jumping jacks on runway. the olympics have been cancelled in his honor

wint
@dril

2288861585018961192

petition to make cvs stop forcing their pharmacists to wear shirts

wint
@dril

979172176598302472

I consider making my posts good a Moral Imperative . I owe it to my follower's to deliver them a product completely devoid of Nude imagery .

wint
@dril

9040823350664415106

wearing my lab coat and analyzing an array of my own nudes in order to determine which one most effectively highlights my fatigued genitals

wint
@dril

390131972116209664

i jsut imagined a nude body and winded my self

wint
@dril

2975075946665345024

**wint**
@dril

fucking Nude Man ruine all our laser tag games, cant shoot him cause he isnt wearing the vest, cant rack up any points against him

1781915399959377920

**wint**
@dril

a cement truck pouring its load on a bare ass nude man lying face down while people sing happy birthday to him

530401684884041728

**wint**
@dril

id say my most defining quality is that i instinctively write tremendous amounts of think pieces whenever i see a naked person

660640994724048896

**wint**
@dril

"clothes" are a construct you fucking dolt. as well as flintsonte chewable vitamins is a construct, and grandmas house is a construct, prick

2472190208294297760

**wint**
@dril

has anyone ever done a powerpoint presentation nude

163881381611585536

the absolute best place to hide your nudes is in a file folder on your desktop labelled "Clothes"

wint
@dril

379530853191139328

a very nude, very fat pink man rolling down the corridors of an ancient temple, gathering dust and dirt like breadcrumbs on a chicken cutlet

wint
@dril

278535707516100608

whenever i get nude for any reason i hear the dogs go wild outside. must sense something that humans can not.

wint
@dril

170670490128625665

trapped, fully nude, in restaurant bathroom. boss & his wife will be here in 10mins. trying to see if i can make a tuxedo out of tolet paper

wint
@dril

817943976586186753

guess who just filled his hot tub with high fructose corn syrup and is ready to take one swee t dip..............

wint
@dril

214186417176330241

wint
@dril

i don't believe in religious, but i respect the fear of nudity

417487967578378240

wint
@dril

the classics(art carney, sid caesar) woud SHIT THEMSELVES if they saw these newer performers who INSIST on displaying their genitals always,

357198672833941504

wint
@dril

buried in the center of stonehenge is a leather portfolio case filled with nude images of me. i consider these my most powerful nudes

370518484137951232

wint
@dril

in honorable protest, i will abuse my ass cheeks with radio waves until the Olympics forces all of the swimmers to wear shirts

554922222847287296

wint
@dril

apparently shirtless people are interacting with me on this site. please put on a tasteful button-down top if you want to fav or retweet me.

324543078897684481

"obama needs to stop writing constitutions or whatever and help my failing business sell rat hair to imbeciles"

wint
@dril

wish Obama would authorize some drone strikes against my ex-wife! *the act takes a more serious tone* Instead of doing Benghazi.

335373338530684929

wint
@dril

i siad jobs plan, not inside jobs plan!! #oboama911

112909631675834368

wint
@dril

*hangs political cartoon of obama eating The Jobs with a fork and knife up on the office billboard* you see that? ?? hes esating the jobs.

387567928024899584

wint
@dril

"tthis is some superbly phenomenal shit." -spoken by president barack obama, upon following his 650,000th twitter account

418042500574486529

wint
@dril

%%%% the arab prince of hell obama dances in front of his throne while controlling the death markets with his enchanted baton %%%%

241670667068661761

reviewed obama inauguration speech. not ONE mention of "varmints" #ProVarmintPres?? #getUmOut

wint
@dril

297394196535468032

"your posts, they aren't good." obama told me over his personal phone line. "you have to put down the keyboard. you have to #StopThePosts".

wint
@dril

402800098612367360

im not saying the release of my FF6 Nude Mod incrased obamas approval rating, but there's certainly a correlation that's difficult to ignore

wint
@dril

131264533703557120

im little jesica. im dying because of obamas help care bill. im on my death bed and the doctor is ignoring me because my dady works hard

wint
@dril

11074098650

president obama orders assassination of the man who holds a "COWBOY ISNT REAL" sign outside of the longhorn steakhouse

wint
@dril

216619255322525696

wint
@dril

me and six or seven other worked up, wild eyed heteros are gonna bust up a gas station with grappling hooks to protest obamas new hoagie tax

2447956449617767425

wint
@dril

obama and his crack team of nsa crooks watching me shit: "sir, he's scooting backwards so his dick doesn't touch the rim" "Thuis guy's good"

3449419233351527424

*"sorry boys.. im goin A.W.O.L.. !!!*
*Another Weekend On-Line"*

i fucking love logging in and out of things at incredible speed

wint
@dril

5478784610254479937

first day i got online on a man named Mumbai_Eddie accused me of having diarrhea, so i detached my modem and put it in the sink for 8 years

wint
@dril

6910954141210460017

i just found The Dos Equis Most Interesting Man In The World's deviant art account. he draws his own jeff dunham puppets

wint
@dril

9749824463609446464

makimg a Meme Quilt, where we send a quilt all over the world & each person adds a patch featuring their favorite online meme . a bit of fun

wint
@dril

5450407516008816464

well im sad to announce that the meme quilt project has been cancelled. someone has already jacked off on it instead of adding their patch

wint
@dril

5450408645828567004

GagBlog.Eu // 12 Most Awkward Honor Killings // The Ten Beer Commandments // Sex Mom Debunks LIBOR Scandal // GagBlog.Eu

wint
@dril

2315874496698286 10

NASCAR Forums >> Odds & Ends >> what are some good podcasts to listen to while listlessly fucking my wife

wint
@dril

3768362163745 83297

"the online web. truly a touching testament to the power of... deeply Human connections." -what Abe Lincoln would say if he were alive still

wint
@dril

6018573703403 39713

forum gods:
1) the guy who dug a big hole in his basement & posted pictures of the hole
2) the guy who intentionally gave his wife head lice

wint
@dril

8496671057295 03232

while you all dunce around here and kiss the stupid royal baby's dick; i'll be absorbing the scooby doo subreddit with a glass of #PaleAle .

wint
@dril

3593086453406 92480

there were 100 browser games in the 2000s where the goal was to become a Pimp by sending links to people, but thats jsut real life now

wint
@dril

973264862158774272

 CRASHED RECUMBENT BIKE IN2 SOME FUCKED UP BRAMBLE PATCH WHILE TAKING PICS OF HANGNAIL FOR WIKIPEDIA. MY CRIES FOR HELP ARE MUFFLED BY MY ASS

wint
@dril

222316334552317952

 hm lets see.. *Logs On To Dark Net* bomb recipes... voyeur upskirt.. snuff vids.. DILBERT?? WHo thef fuck put dilbert on dark net

wint
@dril

35713808747986944

 WHAT DO WE WANT
"Memes"
WHEN DO WE WANT IT
"Instead of regular jokes"

wint
@dril

358998221168709632

 i saw a man at rofl con with a huge black stain down the ass crack. can another attendee please confirm #roflcon #StainMan

wint
@dril

198887469507289088

reddit: my uncle caught me licking my sistser's bicycle seat and now i need u to send me as many mcdonald's monopoly game pieces as possible

wint
@dril

2162070254460363264

who the fuck is scraeming "LOG OFF" at my house. show yourself, coward. i will never log off

wint
@dril

2472223603091121024

i spend the majority of my computer time #Frowning

wint
@dril

3665610061111043584

once a year on every forum some guy posts a thread called like "Im done with wiping my ass" and all the people who get mad at him are banned

wint
@dril

8896428296261877776

i jsut made $9 on amazon's Mechanical Turk after clicking on pictures of Silos for 30 hours straight., eat my shit #goingGolt #JOhngolt

wint
@dril

2222200554411294208

bewildered by this one star review of a pocket pussy from a verified buyer that is just the word "Stupid"

wint
@dril

920749228351246338

b3ndr, PepsiCynic, and myself will be streaming an incan healing ritual, intending to absorb blood from viewers to regenerate our foreskins

wint
@dril

207486741194608640

Whats great is I can get online & read 100 peoples opinions about Kevlar Vests, and at least 2 of them are guaranteed to be probably correct

wint
@dril

943648283599220738

the next big online thing is men who eat Dog Food, schedule meetups to eat dog food together and form rivalries with cat & baby food eaters

wint
@dril

314050982709440512

attention all cops on reddit who have murdered people ; was it Awkward? what gun did you use. did you get a promotion

wint
@dril

477676265458384896

((sends yoyu an unsolicited 20 image sequence of me morphing into a neopet) i can take u... closer

wint
@dril

5357942362818682 88

*understands tthe full potential of the net all at once and stumbles backward wwhile struggling to breathe* christ,. my god

wint
@dril

4485710600119255 04

for each day that Arbys.com does not return the Frames Version of their website I will go to Petsmart and kill one beautiful bird

wint
@dril

1536060648462827 53

i would advise U not to visit this small minded website, MEETUP.COM; They get mad if yo[u bring devil sticks to the meetups even if your pro

wint
@dril

1199710524482641 92

darknet 2002: pics of dead guys in bath tubs, warez
darknet 2017: discussions amongst the boys as to which of our acquaintances aren t funny

wint
@dril

8960738087375872 00

released statement regarding Grumpy Cat urinary tract infection: "Grumpy Cat is in a lot of pain, but still wants to entertain you at shows"

wint
@dril

634701155600330752

i got lock jaw from eating pasta out of a dogbowl and my wife will be here in 2 hours to marry me. help me github

wint
@dril

793609053586980864

wassup babe, im the reason Pregnancy-info .net disabled video embedding on their forums, how abuot giving me a nice kiss

wint
@dril

206049272582512640

well i was going to climb mount everest but this yelp review says theres a nude man at the summit swinging chains around and yelling "fuck u

wint
@dril

216036653423267841

scribbling my exposed dick out of this photo with a blue bic pen so its good enough for linked in

wint
@dril

816669429006073856

wint
@dril

to the coward fraud who claimed my username: it is you who deserves to be plagued by this baneful "2". Posted by CrotchLordMiami2 at 3:36 am

157474733749837826

wint
@dril

will no longer be livestreaming foreskin restoration process; the trolls who attempted to summon [インプ] (Imps) into the chatroom are to blame

1655260846648279904

*"The b est shit I ever did was shatter all the windows in a room just by doing a perfect somersault"*

my grave is just a huge tv displaying videos of me doing parkour in hell and it makes all the other graves look like shit

wint
@dril

381541929554440192

THE MASTER: LETS SEE U DO SOME SICK PARKOUR OFF OF... THIS!! *REVEALS ENORMOUS BANANA PEEL*

wint
@dril

28560030990

turn on c-span, therse a man with an anonymous mask doing parkour on the senate floor and im rubbing my face on the tv to absorb his energy

wint
@dril

203846294983282688

senator rich blumenthal (D-CT) just threw a towel over the parkour mans head. game over, earth is dead

wint
@dril

203851540014960640

closing off this childrens' playground until i am done filming parkour montage which i will use as psychological warfare against my landlord

wint
@dril

2433635786617401347

"i'm sorry but can you please remove the pig display at the zoo. nobody comes to the zoo to see pigs. what the fuck is wrong with you."

it is unfair that i should have to go to hell just because i was born with a pigs brain

wint
@dril

4357174402074882880

pig nosed man arrested for trying to whisk an egg using his fingers

wint
@dril

8240633978221236322

please let me edit my tweets so i can go back and remove every reference to pig piss and liking pig piss

wint
@dril

4348620331592113058

i have a rare condition which is commonly known a s "pig ear", and if I was born in the 1950s i would have been euthanized #Blessed

wint
@dril

275931161908371457

pigmail will replace email in 2010

wint
@dril

15794792410

can 1000000 irate south korean pigs buried alive after a foot and mouth outbreak possibly join forces and cause an 8.9 eartquake??? #yes

wint
@dril

47318132943110144

i do not 'Get' porky pig

wint
@dril

8987847938118791936

shit head with hog DNA takes cardboard pennzoil display hostage

wint
@dril

5508239549913121896

"im the guy who is famous at the hospital because i had to have two catheters put in since i piss so much"

you see; most of the piss were exposed to in our day-to-day lives is immediately diluted by toilet water. pure piss is a monster all its own

wint
@dril

5508703491315548 16

listen fuck wit. if you dont want me pissng all down the floor and the walls of your public restroom then make the urinals. bigger

wint
@dril

703141889357139968

as torrents of horse piss splatter clamorously onto my forehead I scream in absolute torment but make no attempt to move or cover my face

wint
@dril

474218367059247105

i have been tasting my piss every day in order to develop an immunity to it. i am immune to piss. if you piss on me ill just laugh at you.

wint
@dril

134941998493876225

a sterling silver olympic trophy filled with piss labeled "My Death"

wint
@dril

16418065462

wint @dril

once inside the Visitor base i stood before their marvelous spacecraft and covered it with my piss. my god. my god. my god #VANGUARDSOF2012

10256067321659392

 wint @dril

accidentally brought my piss detector into the mens room again and cowered beneath a sink as the deafening screech echoed off the hard tile

683033164651073536

 wint @dril

im about to get my piss tested for steroids. if they find steroids in there then ill start drinking it instead of going to the steroid store

5137075071316213 76

 wint @dril

TODAY: - pissed some body off
- got my ass kicked
- Pissed myself
- got piss kicked into my ass
- ANd its only 2:01 AM.

1010765087521505281

 wint @dril

bathrooms in japan have virtually no piss on them. this is because the culture has instilled a sens e of humility within the people. no piss

289533598640504832

im a tennis ball and my primary mode of transportation is being pushed around by animal piss

wint
@dril

181593656950669312

if all the girls and women in this town want to secretly film me taking a huge piss, then that's their right and god bless em

wint
@dril

381445716964429825

i hand the doctor my urine sample and he removes a tiny wad of flesh floating around in it. "i believe this is yours" "yeah that's my dick"

wint
@dril

218876334573764609

"*cops should have two guns to get rid of crime faster . cops should be dual wielding by 2016*"

cops need grenades. doinate all of your hand grenades to the local police force or face insane cop torture forever

wint
@dril

453083105323409408

if the state ordered me to wear one of those shitty lapel cams i'd say "No SIR" & crush the camera under my cop boot while the public cheers

wint
@dril

397591271889317889

really lookjing forward to going through puberty again and becoming a cop

wint
@dril

510938635659919360

- ass kicked in hooters parking lot - thinks thunder storms are fake - donated 200 Emeralds to the police

wint
@dril

911273665001598976

reminder to all of my female cop followers that i worship female cops daily

wint
@dril

392929829604962305

"hello 911 I need a moat dug around my house immediately"
"sir this line is for emergencies only"
"Thuis is an emergency moat"

wint
@dril

468158810356322305

a bunch of cops knock my colostomy bag on the floor and begin stepping on it with high heeled shoes while i jack off and ask them to stop it

wint
@dril

317953710821097473

a cop will spank you publicly just for breast feeding your pitbull in public . but when a bug bites you hes all "euhhh i dont arrest bugs"

wint
@dril

237065379179003904

lets set some realistic goals here : jokes banned by 2016. sex banned by 2020. a cop in every household by 2025

wint
@dril

372720390369726465

sorry to all crooks, hucksters, cronies, and phonies... but in this, our year of 2016, police man is sitll king, and the jail, his Kingdom !

wint
@dril

7032712256746637312

i shsould be allowed to beat off in the back of a police car. im already going to jail so whats the difference

wint
@dril

857850429027287O5

i will never apologize for accidentally dialing 911 in my jeans pocket or accidentally begging the operator for a "cop massage"

wint
@dril

314004272335433728

u know irt's a Monday when you rear-end a cop car and your trunk pops open, launching 500 or so jars of piss onto another cop car behind you

wint
@dril

463345799913406464

(cop inspecting his new body cam with huge pepperoni fingers) what the fuck is htis. where do i pack the ammo. is this a new type of grenade

wint
@dril

539657944833732608

it may seem that cops are all fucking dumb, bad at IQ tests, etc, but they only pretend to be, to lull crooks into a false sense of security

wint
@dril

770640293423185920

"humankind is so corrupt" i mutter as i sandwich my dick between my badge and gun and take several pics of it with a disposable camera

2060564048454477888

man on mountaintop wont stop yelling "Wanker" , cops cannot reach him buecause of falling rocks

211656836926021633

i think police should get extensive background checks so that i can hire all fo the most insane, mentally ill cops as my personal bodyguards

496072540482453504

((restrained by cops and forced to watch a man put mustard on a bagel) nno!! you're ruining it! That's quality bakedgoods

585458361614864384

(bored in apartment on two week administrative leave after nuking a 14 year old girl with a napalm launcher) THIS FUCKIN SUX !!!!!

465537868660998144

wint @dril

wint
@dril

police man kicks me in the diaper while running out of radio shack, causing my shit 2 fountain up and ruin several RC spongebobs #rodneyking

59069959921336320

"*Politic's is back baby. It's good again. Awoouu (wolf Howl)*"

**wint**
@dril

2020: america elects the first Shirtless president

218431733224325121

**wint**
@dril

donald trump has no time to fuck. he looks at his watch and says "i could not possibly fuck at this juncture." as he powerwalks into the zoo

4617611941443305152

**wint**
@dril

Mahmoud Ahmadinejad Has A New Wine Out. I'm Dying To Try It But I Find His Governing Policies Questionable At Best. Such Is My Life Of Shit.

3004738728879345665

**wint**
@dril

the most fucked up thing saddam hussein ever did was eat doritos in jail

4145243333067743232

**wint**
@dril

i am a local politician and i just want to lick this fucking ridiculous huge lollipop without people photographing me and ruining my career

468879917846134784

came outside today to notice m y "Bring Back The Marriage Ref" bumper sticker violently ripped off. Obviously, I hit a nerve.

wint @dril

102391495021166592

I LOVE TO ROUGHHOUSE , IM A STRAIGHT TICKET VOTER FOR THE GRAVEROBBER PARTY,AND I BELIEVE THE NUMBER ONE ISSUE IS "MOMS AT THE PUMP"

wint @dril

249031310692192258

allow me to reiterate.. im on the side that is the least mad. whichever one that is right now. nobody knows whos more mad at this point.

wint @dril

524206041639440384

congress: it would be an honor to let you join Congress
me: absolutely no. it'd be a disservice to my followers to join the bastard congress

wint @dril

531482937133633538

congress: youre so good at saying the truthful things in a handsome way. we need you
me: Wheres bigfoot. Assholes

wint @dril

531483350725574656

my intense belief: you should not be eligible for the presidency of the United States until you are at least 89 years old

wint
@dril

5376625927106109444

someobdy on here just sent "the cup of stfu" to isis and all of the mainstream media outlets are refusing to report it

wint
@dril

819401128525885441

"For years many have wondered what the letters 'DC' in washington DC stand for. The answer is quite simple: Dollars & CEnts"— Winnie the Pooh

wint
@dril

8721805172858883905

youve heard of the trail of tears, well, if the boys in the white house had their way it would be the trail of taxes, and we;d get the shaft

wint
@dril

568322764052008960

i think it is good to vote, unless it is inconvenient, or boring to do so. then it might be very bad. i'm sorry for doing politics om here.

wint
@dril

529679243060719616

**wint**
@dril

IM AN incest-libertarikin transvaginal ultrasound who owns GUn's and i will post a picture of my dick everyday until voting is made illegal

224154175376859136

**wint**
@dril

obama accuses romney of being unfunny, and too "Random". romney responds by saying obama'/s "Mad" and his page has too much anime shit on it

232111024805912576

**wint**
@dril

sick of seeing "Snark" on my feed regarding our nation's presidential candidates. i will be voting for all of them because they seem nice

690778733897216001

**wint**
@dril

thinking of wrapping my entire body in barbed wire and becoming Sovereign

955106867784626177

**wint**
@dril

nerd with lame attitude: North Korea is bad
Me: Have you ever lived there.
nerd: (his glasses fall off)
Me: Catch you later

496077711434330113

**wint**
**@dril**

my father got sick of wegmans constantly running out of reddi-wip so he started a militia. guess i gotta join his shitty militia now

20793750397652992

**wint**
**@dril**

me and a bunch of stupid assholes are going to start a community in the middle of the desert to either die or prove a very important point

435373709344251904

**wint**
**@dril**

isis man: please! you gotta follow back! you just gotta!
me: no can do my man. i respect your right to be in isis, but I can not follow you.

554689301867683840

**wint**
**@dril**

i proudly skim the amount of $17.76 off of all my employees paychecks, because they do deserve pain

1010451362952433664

**wint**
**@dril**

the facts are thuis: i accidentally did benghazi while trying to steal nfl broadcasts and im sorry about it. this is a stressful year for me

408605108604125184

what if "DONALD TRUMP" was the ceo of NetFlix? I think itd go a little something like this...! (gestures racistly) What a world What a world

wint
@dril

655055062629261312

friday night gathering up together a big pile of things i like to respect (flags, crucifixes ,etc) and just roll around in it ,give kisses,

wint
@dril

7700705936979972224

thats right bitch. i single handedly rescued the constitution of the united states...AND I DID IT WITH OUT USING POLITICS !!

wint
@dril

9765753257781012485

@realDonaldTrump my car has a beehive somewhere inside of it and i think "the donald" should fire it

wint
@dril

399182545192902659

bush was the president who likes oil. correct? so what i think is that its actually "Castor oil", because he leaves a bad taste in my mout!!

wint
@dril

634195596837036033

year 2160 - the huggies corporation pays the united states govt 4 quadrillion dollars to suppress socialized sewage treatment

wint
@dril

22358828729245697

if you odn't subscribe to every last one of my vague, yet cocksure beliefs regarding the Portuguese , i will never make eye contact with you

wint
@dril

6177796909357363200

$1000000 Post: julian assange walking out of the ecuadoran embassy covered in shit and saying do not go in there like ace ventuera

wint
@dril

1025035968904974337

ill vote for the candidate who promises to make masturbating in haunted houses illegal

wint
@dril

15947764973

tried to take two screaming border collies into voting booth & some 90yr old election official fought me& yanked my pants off. fuck voter id

wint
@dril

261918077380358145

wint
@dril

WHAT ABOut MY FREE SPEECH *a bunch of child porn spills outof mouth* IM AS HUMAN AS THE REST OF U *Dick Flies Out Of Pants And Spins Around*

168934801829666817

 wint
@dril

just had to click down the 4th post today about our mr. president's "thick hooters". lets clear off the bathroom mouth

846011228019441665

 wint
@dril

donlad trump reportedly says that normal type pokemon are a waste of time. they're just dirty birds & rats who have no right being a pokemon

615199946980110336

 wint
@dril

im kel from kenan and kel show. support rand paul for senate or ill put the screw in the tunna.

20929161904

 wint
@dril

here are this year's Vote Multiplers for election day. no, they do not stack
policeman - 10x          army man -12x
verified acct - 15x     Asexual - 18x

795562600788529152

forgetting if "taking the knee" is good or bad relative ot my belief system but getting pissed off at every mention of knees just to be safe

wint
@dril

1010478540968660993

"Is Wario A Libertarian" - the greatest thread in the history of forums, locked by a moderator after 12,239 pages of heated debate,

wint
@dril

107911000199671808

in Are society, women are constantly fucked and had sex with . it is therefore my duty as a Senator to inspect their pussys for microchips

wint
@dril

237594538598862848

(struggling))ok i figured it out: all opinions are good, except for the opinions that say other peoples opinions are bad, because thats rude

wint
@dril

553262252879781888

first you have democrats and rtepublicans. theyre basically the same thing. then you have green party and uh, the whigs. theyre the same too

wint
@dril

713326612100591616

**wint** @dril

let's leave politics in the hog pen and debate the real shit, like which 90yr old restaurant owner invented the original chicken cheesesteak

5731728239314124804

 **wint** @dril

issuing correction on a previous post of mine, regarding the terror group ISIL. you do not, under any circumstances, "gotta hand it to them"

831805955402776576

 **wint** @dril

be warned america. 1st they get us fired from amtrak for saying jacking off in the control car is good, next they start poisoning our wendys

833951887430926337

 **wint** @dril

Donald Fump. Poop fuck

864373467063431169

*"it warms my heart when i see people of every race and creed, setting aside their differences in order to spew piss into my cage and scare me"*

i have black friends. i own all 3 current-gen consoles. my shelves are filled with a variety of Book`s. im virtually untouchable

wint
@dril

16257476393

i did not say that the kid from jungle 2 jungle should be sent to Guantanamo bay, i just said it wouldn't be racist if he was

wint
@dril

7188540147382800449

the us census has analyzed 100 million diapers and figured out which race has the worst smelling turds ,making live leak comments obsolete

wint
@dril

8595863095000932097

thinking back to it.. most slaves, only had to deal with one master. the Modern Content Producer has it far wrose, having to please millions

wint
@dril

85581115680355559424

dont trust the dna tests. i determine my ancestry by looking at a bunch of racist cartoon characters to see which ones piss me off the most

wint
@dril

988863765109145607

#ZodiacFacts black people are all #Gemini

wint
@dril

11723689114

TO AVOID SCARING OR OFFENDING
CHILDREN WE'VE TAKEN ANNE FRANK'S
DIARY AND REPLACED EVERY INSTANCE OF
THE WORD "NAZI" WITH "POLICE MAN"

wint
@dril

45127744954187777

i refuse to consume any product that has
been created by, or is claimed to have been
created by, the ((((Keebler Elves)))

wint
@dril

7478225490069926400

feeling devilishly Racist today... might apply
just a smidgen of Blackface before i go out
chasing cars

wint
@dril

633721638266228736

i weawr blackface while i game to improve
performance. i have no intention of racist.
That will be the final post before i turn my
phone off

wint
@dril

482994922807513090

**wint**
@dril

trying to heal..... please donate to my go fund me... $10 will make me less racist... $100 will make me extremely less racist... thank you...

749438005706883072

**wint**
@dril

turning a big dial taht says "Racism" on it and constantly looking back at the audience for approval like a contestant on the price is right

841892608788041732

**wint**
@dril

*waches the Race War unfold in filthy computer chair, multiple tabs open, cnn msnbc, gawkrer, salon, milk duds** now THis is some good shit,

357324593226194944

**wint**
@dril

winner of this year's prom theme is "shit to israel", with a grand total of 2 votes

187387264110825474

**wint**
@dril

going to start thinking it's " Not a good look" to order 1000 island dressing without being able to name the 1000 islands

873275013272670209

listening to the song "Shortnin Bread" on repeat 7 hours a day and forming some very complicated opinions upon Race

wint
@dril

963058490796380160

people on here treat me like dirt , thats fine, meanwhile hundreds of teens are allowed to go to prom racistly every day

wint
@dril

992708075256762371

bet yoyu think youd never find a mother fucker like me at a primarily Black church. but i like to go,.. just to Smile.. bask in the Energy..

wint
@dril

772134726383599616

top complaints im working on:
- the racism ( of course)
-posting the same shit over & over for years
-not posting enough of the classic shit

wint
@dril

858827830989389824

my followers know i Abhor racism, but i especially dont agree with the thing from old cartoons where black people have dice for teeth

wint
@dril

928655485930295296

wint
@dril

shocking: "racism is the light of my soul. racism is the air that i breathe, and racism is what i like." -RacismMario @CNN @MSNBC @FoxNews

564570300336308225

wint
@dril

painting an exquisite 12 foot mural of martin luther king jr dressed as a cop, entitled "The Dream Realised", to prove im not racist at last

608302147315331072

wint
@dril

thinking of abandoning dreams of becoming a Senator, so i can post about yelling "Fuck" in the bathroom because i accidentally became racist

921836965317799937

wint
@dril

the bobs big boy milkshake mix up has become Racial.  i repeat, the bobs big boy milkshake mix up has become Racial.

1027759044415512577

wint
@dril

my name is WhiteMadeaFan55 and i demand ansers.

386231556110422016

"im the only guy who knows how to call out the bull shit of society the smart way. and against all odds i do it for free"

PEOPLE MAG: which pop culture icon are u going to Slaughter next...
ME: I have set my sights on "The Boogie Woogie Bugle Boy of Company B."

wint
@dril

840068779375702017

and folks.. we cant forget aobut Tennis Shoes (Audience boos.) Are you Tennis, or are you shoes? Who'd'y'a'think'ya're ? (Applause)

wint
@dril

615635466252079104

whats the deal with people handing me receipts after i buy things!! i dont want this!! fuck you!! fuck you!! fuck you!! fuck you! #Stand #Up

wint
@dril

336951583629799424

Starfish Rant. ive had it up to here with this bullshit animal. click here to watch my starfish rant

wint
@dril

167658287108599809

llove "Driving Um Wild" with my trade mark wrong opinions

wint
@dril

608101661328973824

wint
@dril

Shut the fuck up? Now ? Whil;e im smack in the middle of perhaps my most ruthless tear against Netflix Culture? Muwahaha. Never

640726844153724929

wint
@dril

the times they are indeed a changin..but the one time thatll never change is Lunch time. lock them engagements in if you think this is good.

660986504261599235

wint
@dril

THINKING ABOUT WHEN DID "IN GOD WE TRUST" BECOME " WOULD YOU LIKE FRIES WITH THAT"

692691653673492480

wint
@dril

life is aobut too many chairs. you got the tv chair, dinner table chair, the dentists chair, electric chair... thats too many. Tone it down

686258043747733505

wint
@dril

i love being the guy at pitch fork whose job it is to argue that thr greatest song of all time is "You Aint Nothin But A Hound Dog" by elvis

1027186655919190016

no!! all of you, stotp it!! please! the insight is too Raw!!

wint
@dril

989734103394750464

There's no greater television program than The News. The News is the only show on TV that I like, and it's smart. #TheThursdayNiteRant

wint
@dril

396051330055159808

whos gonna rake all these leaves up?? the police? #TheThursdayNiteRant

wint
@dril

393565775446814721

alright shit for brain listen up. i dont want this guacamole stuff youre peddling. its green and it looks sick. go home #TheThursdayNiteRant

wint
@dril

390961510991687680

my blood glucose test strip unboxing video maintains a remarkable zero views despite me spending $8000 on Media courses #TheThursdayNiteRat

wint
@dril

403672158477361152

**wint**
@dril

this website seems more & more like a place where elitist daddys boys can show off how 'CLEVER" they are, instead of a source for bra advice

677831655592185856

**wint**
@dril

"cmon!! post it!"
Oh no, i couldnt possibly. Its too fucked up. Too raw
"cmon!! ya gotta post it!"
Very well: NHL Players should wear hijabs

958121294221934592

**wint**
@dril

*steps up to mic; booed immediately* geico commericals are tthis generation's pink floyd **boos get louder** can anyone help me find my car

556515001801125888

**wint**
@dril

the knock out game is a lot of crap. Lord heal oru youth . Lord heal our youth #TheThursdayNiteRant

408804675400392704

**wint**
@dril

hey uh, it's just the thursday nite rant. if youre offended i dont give a shit. Thats whats to be expected from the thurdsay night rant.

390963280006488065

**wint**
**@dril**

15 years ago the most shocking thing online was a picture of a man spreading his ass cheeks open. today, it's my opinions about Wet shaving

638023092334403584

**wint**
**@dril**

ah, So u persecute Jared Fogle just because he has different beliefs? Do Tell. (girls get mad at me) Sorry. Im sorry. Im trying to remove it

660644922744262656

**wint**
**@dril**

time for another rant. fuck igloos. shitty ice house.s too cold. for more rants check out my site. send paypal to theloneranter@rantman.com

272892102340395008

**wint**
**@dril**

if you have ever disagreed with anyone about anything youre a sociopathic piece of shit

331210528183697409

**wint**
**@dril**

ruinning a mans wedding by using too many ad Hominem arguments

1002717483491643392

"*purchased a cage full of rats in the hope that infusing my home with New Life will fire up my posts a nd score me the Bertucci's deal. amen*"

reading my revolting tweets to a focus group for several hours and escaping on a sled pulled by rats when it is time to pay each of them $25

wint
@dril

304684757537669121

the asimo robot is full of rats. nobody ever washes it

wint
@dril

453235830392631296

please bring your rats to the new castle flea market so I may bless/heal them. ill be sitting in a lawn chair wearing a stolen priest outfit

wint
@dril

719432119022403584

stay at home rat

wint
@dril

1028271973674049537

$5 poison vs $100,000 poison.. which kills more Rats

wint
@dril

986412537020284928

wint @dril

NO I WILL NOT USE MY BRAND NEW 3D PRINTER TO PRINT OUT "A PICTURE OF RATS". PLEASE SUGGEST SOMETHING GOOD, LIKE CUSTOM MONOPOLY PIECES

537257597993496577

 wint @dril

need a virginity restoration spell for rats

16452565313

 wint @dril

fired for "unleashing rats at work" which is bull shit first off because they don't make leashes for rats

420910997633646592

 wint @dril

too many movies about rats

868173249808666625

"i.. im gonna lose it!! im absolutely ready to crap all my damn cum out !!!"

**wint**
**@dril**

a trail of rose petals leads you to a room bathed in warm candlelight. piled on the sofa is every guinness record book published after 2004

1884166682937696257

**wint**
**@dril**

yea everyone called me Dixie Cup for years juts cause I asked if it was alright to use a dixie cup as a condom in sex ed. im cool now though

4307060500023837696

**wint**
**@dril**

iwant to be pummeled with carpet beaters by eastern european grandmas and make big awful clouds of dust

621293354030989312

**wint**
**@dril**

I GOT - SUCKED OFF - AT HISTORIC COLONIAL WILLIAMSBURG

830096249143570434

**wint**
**@dril**

i am legally required b y the state of wyoming to tell all of you that i was caught fucking urinal cakes. i am a urinal cake fucker

931962944491521

people who jack off in the bedroom:
spiritual, harmonious, Attuned
people who jack off in the bathroom:
intellectual, mechanical, productive

wint
@dril

880906490495807488

I WILL NEVER "PIMP"

wint
@dril

886753493620543488

contrary to the lies posted by a certain
MetalGearEric, i know what the word "sex"
means, and i know what the word "poop"
means

wint
@dril

169179554093608961

ENOUGH *Throws All My Jacking Off
Books And Jacking Off Memorabilia Into
The Garbage*

wint
@dril

356837451672715265

"horny" has killed more people than all the
volcanos on earth combined

wint
@dril

687446125457096704

i want to fuck a sheet of paper

wint
@dril

3141685206886664577

The Bayer corporation proved the link between Masturbation and Homosexuality in 1968. Thbe debate is over.

wint
@dril

3575503188660505088

realdoll corporation accidently sent me a Scarecrow... a sign that I should return to the simple life at my uncle's pumpkin farm?? Probably

wint
@dril

184674553392406528

@CBSTweet IVE DISCOVERED ASPHYXIATING MYSELF NOT ONLY ENHANCES ORGASMS BUT ALSO THE INTENSITY AND FREQUENCY OF LAUGHS FROM UR COMEDY LINEUP

wint
@dril

141411300545789952

i f you see a burlap sack hanging off of an overpass with a dick sticking ot of it thats me trying to fuck hurricane sandy

wint
@dril

262556636172939264

im the only lawyer in nyc who will handle your case AND have sex wit h u

wint
@dril

80424664299601921

sex worship i;s a mental condition that is worse than liking the super bowl

wint
@dril

561759148321566720

some simpsons dvds fall outta my velvet robe while pouring my date a drink at my penthouse suite. i bend down to check if they got fucked up

wint
@dril

199395378016169984

pussy log 12.29.11: justin unscrewed the knob from the door to the ladies' room and now the club boys all take turns cradling it

wint
@dril

152678630034653184

if i could only maneuver myself in such a fashion that my dick could fit into the drain of my bathtub id be truly content with my life

wint
@dril

235056546554470400

Louis? gosh, it's been years. it's me, Neal, from Law School. anyway, i got this big juicy onion here, was thinking me and you could fuck it

wint
@dril

2043795135750055360

if youre following me for vids of me smearing chocolate syrup all over my chest. i dont do that anymore, and i suggest u read the holybook .

wint
@dril

3239318971410268816

im the sex principal. i have sex all the time in the techer lounge. i fuck the lady teachers & i fuck the man teachers. im all fat and shit.

wint
@dril

1681530344428399616

another day volunteering at the betsy ross museum. everyone keeps asking me if they can fuck the flag. buddy, they wont even let me fuck it

wint
@dril

1714508353882203008

indonesian pirates raid my yacht and find me on the floor fucking a styrofoam container

wint
@dril

5057689856995655568

dick stuck in a moth ball

wint
@dril

509247353271123968

SEX !!!! !!!! ...now that i have you're attention, here are some pictures of me and my wife having sex

wint
@dril

867440016577798144

rip out my chest hiar and shove fistfuls of it into my fat mouth while my slobber-glazed jowls shake about and sprinkle your bosom with spit

wint
@dril

231178865756762113

rating a porno "thumbs down" just because thegirl wouldnt take off her blue tooth head set is one of the moust fucked up things i ever did .

wint
@dril

282693697106239488

does Theire exist a single caveman who has gained lastable notoriety through his or her accomplishments? Not a one. ban sex and ban caves

wint
@dril

233558173078913024

*"buddy youre ten pounds of shit in a ten pound bag, of shit"*

imagine a world where we could all smell our turds while theyre still in our body. capital one whats in your wallet

8598695154584465792

smear turds all over my dunce cap and kill me

2980897406269685576

i have no idea how that turd got on your ceiling, but it definitely didn't fly out of my shorts while iwas doing a backflip

1829553429955525632

when the doctor ask's you for a stool sample but you dont know how much he needs so you load up like an entire keg with turds "Just in case"

884309595551920128

"big craps are good". never have is een such a foolhardy sentiment expressed on here. "Big craps are good". Absurd. The words make no sense

5357816902923304496

wint
@dril

i;m selling my piss and shit back to the grid

wint
@dril

364326592509521925

nothing like pouring a fresh bag of kitty litter down the ass crack after another liberating diarrhea shit

wint
@dril

577479173897383936

"brevity is the soul of SHIT" - the shit man

wint
@dril

150966198278959106

THE TWIITTER DOT COM PROCESS: THROW PIECES OF SHIT AT THE WALL UNTIL SOMETHING STICKS, EXCEPT INSTEAD OF A WALL IT IS A LARGER PIECE OF SHIT

wint
@dril

884309595551920128

something like 43% of our nations topsoil is actually cave man shit. fucked up

wint
@dril

369355644429549568

the truth is; a lot of these people making and laughing at shit and piss jokes are actually quite stoic when they're using the toilet

wint
@dril

375447484870299648

people come up to me and say, "I will never use the bathroom. I will never shit" and i gotta tell them pal, sooner or later youre gonna shit

wint
@dril

828031141546430465

seems to me i am one of the only people on this earth who knows exactly how high they stack shit.

wint
@dril

990982953445609473

and to the guy who said i have shit for brains: youre right. i do have... four brains..........

wint
@dril

884309595551920128

hello. im calling to report a misprint at the shirt factory. ordered 700 "shit man" tshirts but they all say "shirt man". no i will NOT hold

wint
@dril

246404470370615296

**wint**
**@dril**

let me justt play devil's advocate here and say that eating shit is really good and im a dumb shithead and i love shit

361284669578297344

**wint**
**@dril**

nows the time when the CEO of the company inspects each employee's shit, and im nervous cus my turds look like fucked up little caterpillers

212590528225742849

**wint**
**@dril**

im out here in the yard trying to clean up my turds with a hair brush

588024163358613504

"no"

the much anticipated photographic evidence that i take good care of my gumline has been postponed due to drama and agony

wint
@dril

398353135921401856

I want to be Gargled at. I Want To Be Spit On, Hollered, and Fucked at. I Want To Be Pissed Towards. I Want My God Given Disposal

wint
@dril

2276664501129764353

gah. turned a corner too quickly and maimed my nuts

wint
@dril

881714046445248512

a man in a leather jacket emblazoned with "BabeSmoocher" single handeldly ruined my high school experience and is the reason im unemployed

wint
@dril

250275811884687360

"Ive been studying to become a Pharmacist" Thats good. Im living in one of those crane game enclosures now. Sometimes the claw jacks me off,

wint
@dril

785883554228101122

thinking abou t having a phase in my mid-50s where i wear a whislte every where i go and make everyone around me call me "Coach"

894766999968010240

belittle mme. call me shit. throw hair at me

273274270090661889

university lost accreditation when nickelodeon slimed the dean, degree is useless, 200000 in debt & back in diapers, love getting ass kicked

603681362479026177

im a bush-league yokel who should be put on the floor

636250933245149184

my name is Tony Turds and i demand for people to take me seriously everty time i talk and also for people to like me

367334475216068608

as this website's foremost broken human being, id like to annoucne that oysters make me mad now, for some reason

wint
@dril

5324500003391098880

interstate shut down due to reports of 600 pound man chasing a windswept bra

wint
@dril

9592320162555537153

im stupider then dog shit, i dont give a shit, and i dont give a fuck, and i will never shut the fuck up, and i'll always Respect my enemys.

wint
@dril

9051676929315506177

*inhales sharply and punches a sofa 6 times extremely quickly*

wint
@dril

4195609748882848768

when i cant decide whether to throw up into the trash can or the toilet i throw up in the trash cadn & pour about half of it into the toilet

wint
@dril

4105807356811768832

jacking off more often (due to Stress) and also jacking off less often (due to Stress)

wint
@dril

926579567522918400

im tierd of extroverts crucifying me and my cool introvert friends

wint
@dril

466221533279432704

GET PAID TO CRY - MAKE UP TO "$4.98" A DAY SOBBING ON WEBCAM -MAIL US TEARS FOR ʙᴏɴᴜsʙᴜx®- ABJECT HUMAN MISERY IS THE LIFEBLOOD - DIE A HERO

wint
@dril

314437287465349120

now i will be the first to admit that im an irredeemable son of a bitch/. however, i am also a piece of shit with no brain.

wint
@dril

334560735839535105

driove 5 hours to rodneygamerfield's apartment to sit on his mattress and watch the animatrix while he played on the computer.

wint
@dril

869466392675876864

the numa numa man just bougt a
$70million house and im here at the library
trying to photocopy a fruit roll up

wint
@dril

5460302204918628544

the big seat of my sweat pants sagging
beneath the weight of globs of neosporin as i
waddlle my fuckface ass off to the impound
lot

wint
@dril

6916045656957795200

hate it when my boss knocks out the front
leg of my desk with a baseball bat and funko
pop lego shit flies every where

wint
@dril

9614873718448845568

phaw!! 2am!.. time to go hit the hay (jacks
off and comes back ot the computer)

wint
@dril

618286522773549056

speaking of war crimes, some say the white
flag of surrender was inspired by a piece of
toilet paper dangling pitifully from my ass

wint
@dril

459373515708579840

i tried to drown myself in the toilet but my neck is too big to allow my face to reach the water so now im downloading some nice blogs

wint
@dril

2807086290264391 68

palm thrust my entire head through the fucking wall and kick my big ass while im trapped like a stuck hog

wint
@dril

7912697182042234 89

im sorry to everyone who has ever wanted me to apologize to them for something, and im sorry for apologizing tio you if you didnt need me to

wint
@dril

5367053206856663 04

i can just tell all of you are going to be a bucnh of little shits today and rat fuck me out of another pulitzer price by not retweeting me

wint
@dril

1025043452189233153

"im bad at running and moving around but my upper body speed is incredile" i would like to apologize for letting the team down by eating an entire snowman over the weekend and getting sick. my head wasnt in the game

wint
@dril

4234563724420025984

(pics of hole in wall) thats what happen when i got very pissed off by the sports radio caller saying the football players should run slower

wint
@dril

518555342327017473

thinking of being appointed the official "Bitch" of the NFL

wint
@dril

9688879114113146688

"god damnit!" the coach rips his headset off "they covered our football in nerd cum! those bastards have covered our football in nerd cum!"

wint
@dril

408052812413538305

the crack of the bat. the scent of a verdant field. The excitement of the crowd. These are the things that piss base ball fans off the most

wint
@dril

1008896576876670977

the basketball version of a home run is when you throw a basketball really hard at the roof and get it stuck in the rafters some how

wint
@dril

1001507248747827200

brett favre punches a curtain with the word "INCEST" painted on it, rips it down, looks into cam and says "No Incest" #PublicService

wint
@dril

56375183337988096

wearing the wrong damn shoes to the basketball court, getting freaked on like a Dunce, getting my ass kicked stupidly

wint
@dril

1004385671803539457

if ur wrestling coach calls himself "mr feet pics" and has pictures of feet all over his office, break his trophies for dishonoring the game

wint
@dril

2145724011164431361

i hate it when the refferree kicks me in the balls and ass while my opponent has me in a head lock

wint
@dril

8308992857430016012

what do I model, you ask? i model for those gag golf trophies that are given to bad players by coworkers as a joke. guy with twisted up club

wint
@dril

297379262070149120

huge tub of au jus sauce with bottles of beer floating around in it is lowered into the room before the big game. "now that's, a power play"

wint
@dril

397425967825551360

i think that the dog version of the super bowl shoyuld show some god damn respect to the regular version of the super bowl

wint
@dril

430074074933366784

flipping your car on purpose is even more of an olympic game, than the actual olympic games

wint
@dril

979147000162799617

i'm not allowed to participate in the olympics this year because i have "no discernible athletic talent" and my "dick looks chewed up"

wint
@dril

429012718398353408

me: i dont even care if they cancel sports
howard stern: Thats wild

**wint**
**@dril**

459523497363271682

it is official. im taking my football to prom
and im going to kiss it and the nerds will
never stop me. i cannot wait to savor their
anguish

**wint**
**@dril**

338379172265209857

i think my goal in life is to start a football
team named "The Baseball Preferrers" and
our gimmick is to get as many penalties as
possible

**wint**
**@dril**

618859303525597184

im one of the best supporters of gay on
this site. but. the top priority of the nba is
putting the numbers up. we cant let players
get horny

**wint**
**@dril**

328933656829763585

how much money would have to be given
to FOX executives in order to make the
dancing football robot say "lets kiss some
nerds dicks" on tv

**wint**
**@dril**

258035231754424320

no. i dont care where you hold the "2012 Incest Olympics" but its not gonna be on my roof

wint
@dril

149375021939310592

i will not close my account until the sport of golf is rightfully named "golfball" like the other ball sports

wint
@dril

619423518032171008

if it werent for the sport of hockey, nobody would give a shit about pucks

wint
@dril

706058439903080448

guess what smart guy. cavemen didn't brush their teeth either, but look how strong they were. they also detested sports

wint
@dril

3346453771108172800

We Live IN A Country Where Football Players Are Given Helmets For Free But I Have To Buy A Helmet At The Store Because Im A Regular Person .

wint
@dril

5291618883023335424

"*i believe we gotta push forward and afford dynamic, web based Content the exact same dignities and legal rights as Human Life*"

my name id yogi. greetings from albania. i would like to put the new i pad in jail. thank you for reading to my message.

wint
@dril

392713154574053376

"RSS FEeds? ", i say as i stroke my goatee while leaning on my podcast's huge 3d logo "Never Heard of UM !!!!!!!!!!!!!"

wint
@dril

281831735677825024

"animaniac_fucker" has posted a touching tribute t o the Rwandan Arby's Bombings, please install your CoolBuxVid Media Enhancer to view it

wint
@dril

212843566672789504

i'm going to beat the shit out of asimo. im gping to knock it on its ass while its trying to use a staircase at a trade show. dreadful beast

wint
@dril

452626436915200000

id like to report an error of the googleglass please. if you accidentally wear it backwards it sends video of a big horrible eye to everyone

wint
@dril

455696383798820864

you see this..? *taps computer monitor with finger* this is not just a bunch of mixed up numbers and digits. this is a kingdom of Minds..

wint
@dril

578187246400065536

i have every net flick

wint
@dril

633110353174511617

i just tattooed a qr code to my ass and when you scan it a picture of my ass comes up

wint
@dril

265319639142240258

i forgot to take off my joke shock ring before jerking off and the joke is on me because i flipped out and shot loads all over my curtains

wint
@dril

384811948207919104

taking sips from a big fat thermos with the isis flag on it. thinking about inventing an app that tells me when lunch time is

wint
@dril

652774690130403328

(speaking into phone) get me on the computer

wint
@dril

925509673272344576

dick stuck in roomba - my dick has become trapped in a roomba, the Bastard of automated cleaning devices - i want 911 please

wint
@dril

237880898358505472

BIGMOUTH BILLYBASS REVIVAL , SINGS GAGA, BIEBER, ET AL; INFUSED WITH 2012 TECH FOR SHIT & PISS CAPABILITIES; "PHENOMENAL" FORBES MAGAZINE

wint
@dril

114833694560235520

the ye.ar is 2009 AD. world government has passed the G.R.E.E.D ACt, banning ownership of CD-ROM. hyperlinks have repleaced the dollar .

wint
@dril

249985527669997568

windows..on behalf of all boys online, INCLUDING the trolls, id like to extend a well-deserve "Thank You" for putting updates in my computer

wint
@dril

633238734838874112

please. look at this thing on my ipod that i loaded up. it is called "the geico talking dog" and it is spectacular. please look. please

wint
@dril

300300203670503425

my true custom rig is a baby grand piano filled with lava lamps

wint
@dril

425911620699561984

if I could only get my Nasty mitts on some HARD-WARE , (RAM , Chips, ) my posts would improve tenfould,

wint
@dril

813357482051600384

My User Experience Conditions - 12/17/17 :
- Will click only 3 links today
- Muting the word "Bluray"
- Unmuting the word "Wendys"

wint
@dril

942503142025056256

Yeah!!! Yeah!!!!!!!!!!!!!! Im Doing it!!! Im experiencing 3d

wint
@dril

16397414991

caught my son running a google search for " shit stain pussy ". i am beyond distraught. we are strictly a Bing family

wint
@dril

343519917217296385

just downloaded some of the most all time realistic vagina pics, to my $100 computer

wint
@dril

1010450901687992320

closing my eyes and mentally visuelizing my enemies bodies, in 3d , to analyze them for weak points

wint
@dril

899610408880934912

i want to be wearing google glass when i see my wife in her wedding dress fofr the very first time so i can turn it into a big dorito

wint
@dril

317139936723734528

old screensaver: spinning 3d monolith with my wife on it
new screensaver: marquee that says "Truck Month" regardless of what month it is

wint
@dril

841183514800377857

**wint**
**@dril**

i piss on your little emails

973810026161819648

**wint**
**@dril**

i am nude, shaved, & ready to be submerged within the digital chrysalis where i will generate bigcoins by doing ki warrior poses until i die

3216764427463720966

**wint**
**@dril**

(takes off VR goggles after howling in fetal position for 3hrs while guys in varsity jackets slap the teeth out of my mouth) wow its so good

775486251214536704

**wint**
**@dril**

as the sun consumes the earth i will stand atop the highest mountain with my arms spread wide , shouting "Bring Back Meebo"

211736300741595136

**wint**
**@dril**

im thinking a tiny palm-sized toilet you can just keep on your desk & jack off into would soon become as ubiquitous as the personal computer

872567737457016838

Let 's Fill The Large Hadron Collider With Garbage Now That They Found Their Shitty Particle

wint
@dril

2222309022036631552

i can confirm israeli android os WILL use a gui based on art assets from dreamworks The Croods & that this is exciting news for Crood likers

wint
@dril

3139888788883233792

setting up your own yahoo account is easy! you just click here, and he.. oh no. i just sent 60,000 pictures of my ass to my boss's daughter

wint
@dril

10062469472985089

im going to be very upset if I shell out a thousand big ones for google's glass only for it to be 100% legal for people to do jokes about it

wint
@dril

372719851003191298

4.2 TB of VR compatible slo-mo footage featuring a man with no teeth shooting a bra using a dsr precision sniper rifle and pistol wipping it

wint
@dril

908340998400614400

cursed pair of google glasses adds world star hip hop watermark to everything i look at and cannot be removed from face

348546943187824640

cave man: ou ou ou,. keep net neautral so me can download Porno
Monopoly guy: why not jack off to a Turner Classic Movie instead

941977285980246016

they should make web 2.0 slot machines that show the faces of your loved ones instead of shit like cherrys, the number 7, and the word "Bar"

1027188670111965186

hopping on some tech support forums to accuse people with minor hardware issues of being Mad

751281763876352000

im the guy in the incognito browser icon who jacks off wearing a trenchcoat and sunglasses

553306506377330689

**wint**
**@dril**

i sense that my Zwinky knows when i'm feeling upset. is it possible that Zwinkys operate on a higher level of consciousness than humans? yes

230528968661536771

**wint**
**@dril**

any one who figures out how to breed border collies with the Microsoft Zune needs to hollaer a message at me

53435192106430464

**wint**
**@dril**

nobody seems to realize how many people had to die to bring 3d back to the theaters and its extremely fucked up that interest is waning

235955374405070849

**wint**
**@dril**

my spinning 3d head rises from a dumpster full of discarded shrimp who were born fucked up by the bp oil spill. eeyaaghhHHH!!! im ALIVE baby

245317509857816576

**wint**
**@dril**

i interface the dunston check 's in dvd with the God Processor. a gruesome polygonal ape head welcomes me to dunston world

424654981698822145

big news gang. another A++ app from the theranos company to help me keep track of all my silver ware. let me just say. Wow

**wint**
**@dril**

1011089539601969152

 my setup: 35 monitors arranged around my swivel chair in a circular fashion, imprisoning me forever in a 3d world of sex pics & sports radio

**wint**
**@dril**

275810221765586945

 can anyone link me some good User Agreements to click yes on,

**wint**
**@dril**

933329602298101760

 im the one guy on earth who thought it was cool that google glass would allow you to look at your dick and make it shrink/change colors

**wint**
**@dril**

1004441988417163265

 some people say, normal peoples brains work in 2-D, while famous authors brains work in 3-D...

**wint**
**@dril**

863953626909356034

"i am a Teen and that's somethjing i have to live with for the rest of my life."

wint
@dril

we have just been informed that more and more teens are buying "wax lips" from candy stores. do not be fooled. these are not their real lips

3233794828849668448

wint
@dril

yes, i am a 24 year old man, and yes, i am the one who spraypainted the word "Teen" on the side wall of sleepy's mattress porfessionals.

197365403490590722

wint
@dril

seems to me, life is aoubt "STICKS"
Age: 1-20 : Selfie Stick
Age 21-90: Walking stick

965998285319270402

wint
@dril

let's be real. they should mkae a less ignorant version of the teen choice awards, and i should win one of them for coming up with the idea.

498686135863095296

wint
@dril

in order to get to the bottom of the SEXTING craze, goerge stephanopolis takes a shit on a teens chest #NEWmedia #oldmedia #moralfocus

25111926713

andy rooney hologram crashes coachella 2013 and berates the audience, calling them "rude" and "a disappointment" #awful

wint
@dril

192289941894594562

now youve done it, teens. the official mr bean account is closing because you all kept calling him dad

wint
@dril

613226696263667712

the infamous millennials are more interested in (consults notepad) being nickeled and dimed by the tax man than (squints) distilling vinegar

wint
@dril

628733067461419009

evry young man MUST receive a cupbox at the age of 17 to carry his favorite cups around and to give him a valuable lesson in responsibility

wint
@dril

15858934190

i would like to remind our nation's youth to burn their mcdonald abd burger king cups after use so mobsters cant hide IEDs in them

wint
@dril

529152581336322050

If youre a milennial who doesnt know what a Farm is "You are part of the aids"

wint
@dril

976805877792591872

Teens respond to scorpions. Im bridging the teen reality with ours, through Scorpion Use. Do scorpions need to act rude to be cool? No

wint
@dril

134944865313234944

Top 3 Cuases Of Teen Death:
1. Noise
2. Misbehavior
3. Jeans

wint
@dril

15942186721

stop it Teens. stop grabbing onto my jeans and SKitching me as i try to run away. im a teen too. im one of you

wint
@dril

218896524430688256

the neighborhood teens have left so many burning bags of garbage on my lawn that everyone thinks that this is the place you burn garbage now

wint
@dril

377336602407628800

wint
@dril

Some Teens Don't Think It's 'Hip' To Undergo Female Circumcision. I Think That's Whack.

19521982807

wint
@dril

just like the time my buddy " chustin " Ate Shit on that ramp we made out of horse bones

6457119755

"dr oz tells me on his show that you can just pour a shit load of mouthwash into your laundry instead of wasting money on various detergent's"

wint
@dril

let me tell you exactly why this t-shirt design of the tasmanian devil with angel wings is bullshit. first off, taz is not dead

381470232432234496

wint
@dril

simpsons marches onward into season 394. characters morph into grotesque mockeries over 100s of years. homer advocates cock and ball torture

3555805105581436417

wint
@dril

my pet iguana' s get angry at the same tv shows I do.... wierd but cool

4394043045513138689

wint
@dril

spike tv is showing some good vids of dudes urinating and im stuck here at work yelling at saudi arabians on the phone for $156.00 an hour

499425557156338O737

wint
@dril

daffy and donald duck: "SAME SHIT , DIFFERENT ASS HOLE"

954527135179395072

wint
@dril

TODAY WE EXPLORE THE LINK BETWEEN WIDESPREAD SOIL EROSION IN HAITI AND MY FAVORITE TV SHOWS BECOMING LESS FUNNY

297365065412272129

wint
@dril

I just got word that a disrespectful message towards Dr. Phil has hit Darknet. Users are advised not to download the offending material.

252436492700491776

wint
@dril

big bird was obviously just a man in a suit. but the other ones were too small to contain men. so what the fuck

398879478912258048

wint
@dril

MAINSTREAM: Barney the dinosaur is some good shit. I like it. It's really good. ME: Barney the dinosaur is bunk. This is a show for children

438067852852359168

wint
@dril

i live for the tears of all baby huey fanboys. their suffering is more essential to my being than the blood flowing through my veins

477099281778626560

the villagers gather at the summit to hear my horrendous impersonations of futurama characters and grant me offerings of ivory and fruit

wint
@dril

330452681237876738

((speaking too close to the microphone at press conference)I have never watched a single episode of the Teletubbies. They look like fools

wint
@dril

481789072407404544

spit takes are funny but if you do them in real life people will call you ass hole

wint
@dril

469285074572034048

i maintain that curly is by far the most malignant stooge. without his toxic influence, moe & larry couldve ascended to unfathomable heights

wint
@dril

766824624931745793

when i see people putting up foul language on to the feed, all i can do is laugh, knowing that they will never get their posts read on Ellen

wint
@dril

849636403306790912

wint @dril

sending slowmo footage of my balls undearneath the bathtub faucet being pulverized by the water pressure to ameicas funniest home videos

1014265337293000710

 wint @dril

ellen made me sign some papers and put a big blown up picture of my leathery dick on her show instead of my topical tweet. ellen fooled me

8710557235302563 84

 wint @dril

imagining the guys on Shark Tank laying into the guy who invented the fucking porky pig character "What were you thinking !!"

978021531048660992

 wint @dril

Doctor Who: Fucking athesit piece of shit. Admit god is real NOW*Waterboards him*
Atheist: No!! I dont want to
Dr Who: Im going to kill you

4798440475240816 64

 wint @dril

please stop adding flintstone chewable vitamin commercials to the episode list. they are not real flintstone episodes.

391837831267495936

-the drew carey show forums harbor a subforum named "Hell"
-users are sent there when they absolutely fuck up while talking about drew carey

wint
@dril

821597110692966403

i've just been notified by the oracle that late night personality jay leno is currently in Denim Mode.

wint
@dril

310577432782569472

im near certain there is a hotly contested tug-of-war between fox executives upon the issue of whether or not homer simpson can show his ass

wint
@dril

843671547260915712

elmer fudd with yakuza tattoos. legion of fudd

wint
@dril

979599188647403521

icant come to work today.. on account of JERRY DUTY *SHoves every seinfeld disk into dvd player at once*

wint
@dril

10849247486287872

theme song to Cheers makes every animal in my house howl untikl i fucking lose it and hurl all their cages across th room into an awful pile

wint
@dril

252163680756719617

the most disgusting accounts on here are making claims like, "Fred Flintstone is a pimp" , with zero evidence

wint
@dril

929441250238922754

@cesarmillan PUT MY DICK ON TV

wint
@dril

180754179407626241

man wearing nothting but socks doing back flip kicks into his tv because there are too many batman shows

wint
@dril

528317018291048448

Im goig to drive a nail through my cock to promote ABC's "The Middle"", and I will be paid $18 for doing it.

wint
@dril

474610986994135040

I SUBMERGE MYSELF INTO THE CORE MIND AND CRACK MYSELF INTO THE BIT-WEB, MERGING MY CONSCIOUSNESS WITH ALL 18 EPISODES OF THE GASTINEAU GIRLS

wint
@dril

274416261084106752

OPRAH: Take us back to the time you invented the famous Livestrong Bracelet. ME: well..i was at boston market, just looking at my wrist, and

wint
@dril

6609847343156618304

please watch my realtiy drama"shit eaters" about people who eat shit and are constantly goaded into cyclical arguments with their loved ones

wint
@dril

302308230355374080

as a youth, the boys would laugh at my large ears & call me "The Ears Bastard". but today, I have every epsIode of Sliders at my fingertips.

wint
@dril

279257452619370496

my name is krayg. i am 49 years old. i have forgone all emotion. i am writing this letter to put an end to the tyranny known as Nick Jr

wint
@dril

234646535290380288

**wint**
**@dril**

MOE     Hitler mrudered over 9million people you numbskull
Moe uses the claw of a hammer to yank on Curly's nostrils
CURLY  Nyuuaagghh!!

374562815706554368

**wint**
**@dril**

im afraid i must say that i do not find the mysteries featured on "scooby-doo" challenging enough .

934242047015387136

**wint**
**@dril**

"peppa pig" is the latest children's TV show that my followers cant wait to see ripped to shreds by my high IQ intelligence, live on my feed

515147633045037056

**wint**
**@dril**

FOX Broadcasting calls every artist, writer, lawyer & executive together to conclusively decide which color the Simpsons' nipples should be

268017145139564545

**wint**
**@dril**

reality tv show where we replace one lucky boy's pc gaming chair with a fully functioning toilet. every episode

798865700030976000

"*enjoying some fucked up thoughts of some boys enjoying the real counter culture shit... such as drinking coffee, and being glad it's friday*" what me & the boys enjoy most is going to a home goods store to laugh at all the toilets. saying "haha i really want to shit in there", etc

wint @dril

407667619970293760

THE BOYS: were watching the mr bean episode where you can see his ass. get over here
ME: cant. wifes making me watch mr beans holiday (2007)

wint @dril

875030913104703489

Just met w/ Boys Lunch Club. Seems to me, That we are very pissed off that teen girls would rather kiss, "Soldier Boy," than Actual Soldiers

wint @dril

732346442761834496

pleased to report my custom beer tap that makes a dramatic diarrhea noise while filling the glass is a hit with the boys at the fondue club

wint @dril

522800303209738241

explaining to the boys at the auto shop what the "you know i did it to him" man is iwth the inflection one might use to discipline a child

wint @dril

957320176705384448

**wint**
**@dril**

when one of the boys tells me he has to use the bathroom i inevitably respond with some stupid shit like "Alright, Sounds Good"

1027758463655469056

**wint**
**@dril**

best is when you're shopping for bedsheets and you see one with a lousy thread count and you say to your buddies "this poiece of shit sucks"

332311696712548352

**wint**
**@dril**

me & the booys are riffing on 78 hours of stolen walgreens security cam footage. this guy on here just bought a toilet brush. bitch!! bitch!

5419464439468072960

**wint**
**@dril**

me and the boys have decided that the least gay way of wiping your ass is to dump a quarter bottle of Palmolive Spring Sensations back there

777202110593114112

**wint**
**@dril**

my repulsive cohorts and I are searching the woods for tree sap so we can rub it all over our hands and improve our golf grip

623664714380263426

me & the boys will be holding hands.,
forming a Covenant Ring, to protest girls
who only want to fuck the main pirate from
the pirate movies

wint
@dril

8711716074731115136

oh yeah buddy... i eat birdseed... and
i ain't a FUCKIN bird!! #JustTheGuys
#DamnMenTweets

wint
@dril

3897874355582095360

me and some extremely crude boys in a
pickup truck scream "hipster" at some kid's
lemonade stand then crash into a turtle and
eat shit hard

wint
@dril

3346560030552248320

going ape shit at the gym. rotating in
full 360 degrees with the boys, flawlessly
synchronized

wint
@dril

9354212114116330240

"i despise the toilet. id love nothing more than to kick it through the wall and shatter it into 100 shards of wet porcelain. But i need it"

**wint**
@dril

when you're sitting on the toilet theres a tiny opening between the seat and your dick/ nut area. this is known as "The Daredevil's Spittoon"

7671243421572221897

**wint**
@dril

but enough about my dick. today, I would like to talk to all of you about the Toilet.

4746125505608982528

**wint**
@dril

ddepressed, exhausted imbecile dragging an overturned port-o-john down the interstate, blocking traffic and getting honked at

309525390903361538

**wint**
@dril

breaking down mentally because im all out of toiolet paper and i cannot decide which wendys coupon to wipe my ass with

8144391757055526272

**wint**
@dril

can I get into legal trouble for secretly filming myself on the toilet

448471160947486721

using the toilet when i hear Our national anthem start to play. i do what i must. i stand tall in complete agony; as shit runs down my leg,

wint
@dril

778663853534117888

Im the guy who exclusively wipes his ass with the disposable seat covers

wint
@dril

789388138607210496

the toilet feeler ruins another public restroom with his grubby hands

wint
@dril

184046114289356801

the adrenaline rush i get from posting gives me the energy to walk to the toilet, and the endorphins i get from shitting allow me to post

wint
@dril

622587563216277504

my meme dissertation should be "put into the toilet"?? perhaps the only thing that should be put into the toilet are your harsh criticisms.

wint
@dril

350948945603727360

**wint**
@dril

i did certainly tilt my entire hosue 45 degrees just so i could install a zipline from my orthopedic gamer cushion to the toilet

4806561242956718l0

**wint**
@dril

here i am again, screaming into the toilet, hoping somehow, somewhere, my future wife can hear my soothing voice resonate intot her asshole.

123802418789089280

**wint**
@dril

heads up: they got free toilets at mcdonalds now

4936320779723735O4

**wint**
@dril

hello 911. the toilet seat ripped my loin cloth off again

766338019427291138

"going to the fire station to kick all the firemens asses wearing my fat ass denim overalls"

wint @dril

i love to do bare knuckle brawls and my garage is adorned with various pornos

3768647585084252I7

 wint @dril

bazooka joe... habve you seen this guy. fuck him. he talks shit even though his comic strip is printed on garbage instead of a newspaper

5071441173073428548

 wint @dril

i am a cot and pickin "tells it like it is "son of a bitch

5848486448697650784

 wint @dril

my followeres, who all hate me, and wish to kick my ass, are nobodys, and they lack the combat training to injure me, because theyre infants

6206455494574569440

 wint @dril

i hereby disavow EpicWayne, who now says that my "ears are fucked-up shaped" , and that i "let dildos roll around in the footwell of my car"

9347192031096691393

i would love to lift all of my pathetic, frail followers by the ankles and huck them like tomahawks

wint
@dril

942511197215252480

i love ggetting hazed so i can gain access into this exclusive club of people who have been forced to eat dog shit

wint
@dril

531163215997460480

i just shot a wicked load across the hood of m y dad's monte carlo and i'm feeling hetero as all hell

wint
@dril

360147005147844608

i will say this. when I finally ascend to the final plane of consciousness .nerds will get extremely yelled at

wint
@dril

462228189406691328

if you have a problem with me kissing pictures of Dragons while driving the bus, fight me. i just ate like 30 hotdogs and im near invincible

wint
@dril

291188536395309056

(in forced toughguy voice ) What the fuck is a clove of garlic. Around here we call it piece of garlic

wint
@dril

610458760176234496

"I love the name of honor, more than I fear death." -me to my boss after he found a picture of me with a big shit stain on my sweatpants

wint
@dril

5698944299071165184

Im sorry? Are u "Going in" on me?? Am I being "Gone In" upon just for p osting my time-tested opinions about girls holding forks incorrectly

wint
@dril

6369204424971038720

go ahead. keep screaming "Shut The Fuck Up " at me. it only makes my opinions Worse

wint
@dril

972534838057230336

a man does a wheelie past you in a motorcycle. the back of his jacket says "TAKE DOWN THE POSTS"

wint
@dril

4817771286653217792

**wint**
**@dril**

i have taken my shirt off over 10000 times

622398881096073216

**wint**
**@dril**

everyone on this site thinks they're hard core but i bet if they took poison to weaken their bodies i would win fights against them handily

514697377044000768

**wint**
**@dril**

i fairly tend to use "Sarchasm" to destroy liars mentally, and if that's not yiur cup of tea, i have the 2 words for you which is Suck it !!

600342922228310016

**wint**
**@dril**

i lovoe challenging people on here to Duals and beaning them with a sniper rifle while theyre like fucking with their phone, waiting for me

874386397024718851

**wint**
**@dril**

im good old southern boy and we dont cotton to bollocks .

247948376040148992

grandmom kicked me out of the house because she caught me waterboarding an extremely small man

wint
@dril

502935250482528256

children.. toddlers.. babies..they all got one thing in common. they all truly believe they can kick my ass. but they are Fundamentally Weak

wint
@dril

814437221898010625

climmbing the power lines until i am less pissed off

wint
@dril

508355967248252928

Geting my ass kicked by italian guys in the tiny bathroom at the back of the bus

wint
@dril

943658415892471809

you come on line and challenge me with a user name like "Lesbian Mr. Clean" , i will not respect you, regardless of your skill lefvel

wint
@dril

923437553193246721

wint
@dril

Some may say iim considered, the Bad Boy of controversy

510209660247625731

wint
@dril

howling james dean lookalikes circling their choppers around me, swinging chains while i sit in the gravel and borwse the nintendo 3ds eshop

599928057219162114

wint
@dril

stonehenge actually sucks and i hope someone pushes those rocks the hell over real soon

520617216124145664

wint
@dril

missed connections: the bone - head who dropped an entire slice of pizza on my brand new Craig Martin`s ( wow yourw a tough guy )

9079868259

wint
@dril

(passes a man in a hardhat toiling over a roadside utility cabinet in 100 degree weather in my black convertible) Nice Fedora Dip Shit

618836402759794688

wint
@dril

wiping out an entire archaeological site by drifting in my 1500-ton big rig truck with "piss up my ass bitch boy" on the side in neon lights

559131028250705920

"*may the wind carry my tweets and soothte the sick, the wounded, the downtrodden of both man & beast, across the savage shit earth of trolls,*"

ijust had one Hell of a steak dinner. i wont post specifics regarding the dinner due to trolls but i would like to get this viral please.,

wint
@dril

539086869762691072

lying on my back, screaming like a wildman while my trolls graze my balls with a spinning bicycle tire

wint
@dril

887455306476814336

ok which one of the trolls told some company in Singapore that im interested in bulk purchases of cheap laminate flooring. i demand answers.

wint
@dril

767122057331089408

to whoever changed my background pic to spider man with his dick out, thank you. im keeping it just to make you mad

wint
@dril

440105585464201216

i was so wound up over trolls this morning i forgot to wipe my ass. i pulled my pants up and the shit coalesced into a wad on my lower back.

wint
@dril

654063505910407169

i attribute the complete failure of my brand to the actions of detractors, oor my "trolls", as it were, as well as my own constant fuckups

wint
@dril

473815588503293952

shutting computer down until the shitty moods & attitudes can fuck off., if you need me ill be on my other computer, sititng 60° to my right

wint
@dril

768409611896496128

me: nobody has to get owned today. please, please put down the keyboard and step back 9 year old child: Fuck oyu

wint
@dril

553268372331573248

Piss_089, noted pervert and imbecil,e made the ridiculous claim that i "love touching pieces of trash cans" & that my "gumline is fucked up"

wint
@dril

274680357952032768

i click online expecting praise from mny contemporaries. instead i get an ass pic on my monitor and i immediately start wheezing into my lap

wint
@dril

522556548967841793

hear this trolls: ive been secretly respecting the flag in the privacy of my garage for 12 hrs a day , maxing out its power to insane levels

wint
@dril

912753223118749696

all the trolls talk shit about my profession as an artisan ass wiper. but when they see my fine selection of towels they beg for my services

wint
@dril

328604418528403456

please stop calling my home with fucked up three stooges noises. my nine daughters no longer respect me after seeing me get mad at the phone

wint
@dril

316446318346252288

let me tell you how i deal with Haters. i collect their piss in a jar and keep it next to my monitor. why?? uhrh. i think it makes them mad

wint
@dril

227380502347276288

took some pics of my new satellite dish, but im not posting them until hatred annd cynicism are eradicated

wint
@dril

568325524893900800

confidently reclining in my seat after calling my onlinw adversary a "shitbarn"

wint
@dril

465850179523198977

getting pisse d off imagining my trolls and dissenters crawling around my house in little butler outfits and expecting tips

wint
@dril

9321692836685 04581

i have posted severla high-res images of my teeth & gums for the inspection of the trolls. they will find that they look like a normal man's

wint
@dril

323373936404475904

when people fuck with me on sites i head for the beach and take it out on the crabs. i punch their shitty little bodies, i kick dirt at them

wint
@dril

310898243267596289

blocked. blocked. blocked. youre all blocked. none of you are free of sin

wint
@dril

473706394009759744

I dont appreciate bieng called "The Waterbed Bitch" just because I own a waterbed and post pictures of it daily

wint
@dril

653389943750959104

Rather tiresome that people wiould rather Threadshit my mentions than say, enjoy a whimsical boating tour through the fair canals of Venice.

wint
@dril

746055181956177920

I just got word that the trolls are atempting to change the name of the Stratolaunch LEO aircraft to "The Stalwart Pussy." We must stop them

wint
@dril

871207966216777729

to the trolls: i just bought a 5-pack of Oral-B electric toothbrush heads using points from my Chase Freedom card. could a child do that? no

wint
@dril

378960748929482753

things the trolls won't allow me to have: - the blue check Mark - the 260 characters - a nice plaque that says "twitter power user"

wint
@dril

928254085412859906

i take a vacation to hawaii to relieve myself of the Trolls. a group of hula girls begin beating me up & calling me shit as soon as i arrive

wint
@dril

375396957063098370

i love having molotov cocktails trown at me in the cyber cafe-- not. idiot

wint
@dril

482990006550937600

"The people who say i should get a life are the real ones who should get a life" - Hamdan bin Mohammed Al Maktoum , Crown Prince of Dubai

wint
@dril

957666436897439744

stumbling through war torn syria with my pants down, begging everyone around me not to feed the trolls

wint
@dril

701970509026746373

the only ones authorized to sneak peeks at my dick are 1) my doctor, 2) my dentist, and 3) my lawyer. as for the trolls? No Dice— Bub.

wint
@dril

231579538650447872

id like uh...medium, w/ pepperoni, sausage and onion. just to piss off the trolls. id like a 2-liter of coke to piss off the trolls as well,

wint
@dril

906632021509885953

laying in the submissive position, letting a gang of trolls piss all over me and saying "Im getting too old for this shit" like a bad ass

wint
@dril

874390753212080130

a particularly rude comment i received today has caused me to fill my pants wih shit. i will not glorify the perpetrator by identifying him.

wint
@dril

309071777466810372

after another day of getting Owned by #HateMail and #DeathThreats nothing beats coming home to my policeman wife and getting shot & arrested

wint
@dril

385178754886021120

user named " beavis_sinatra " has been terrorizing me since 2004, by sending me pictures of cups that are too close to the edge of the table

wint
@dril

712394817272160257

*"i don't have time ot actually read you peoples posts, but ive been evaluating your engagement metric's and they look like Shit..."*

in talks with twitter execs to make my account unblockable, and also Worse

wint
@dril

560972275022045185

my favorite feature of this site is absolutely no consequences for my opinions sucking ffucking ass and me being 100% wrong about everything

wint
@dril

898578630367821825

best part of being a #Verified is undoubtedly having cops throw flash grenades through the window of anyone who tweets the word "Ass" at you

wint
@dril

873396133216886784

i have absolutely zero interest in friendship, i have absolutely zero interest in jokes, i am simply here to collect data and earn respect

wint
@dril

377333121554718720

im starting a new feature on twitter called "Are U for Real". Check it out

wint
@dril

224773121608138752

petition to change the twitter bird into a shittier, less noble animal, l ike a pig or an ape

315689399562141696

THERAPIST: your problem is, that youre perfect, and everyone is jealous of your good posts, and that makes you rightfully upset.
ME: I agree

516183352106577920

scrolling down my feed..lauguhing my ass off at my own trade mark "Knee Slappers", my mouth stuffed with bread making beastly noises

580086324809584640

INTERVIEWER: we looked you up. you dont even have a twitter account, which is good
ME: Actually i was suspended for posting "Gumby shit ass"

737711351150284800

overseeing my pages, patiently watching all the guys i follow do their 'Bits' and mentallly assigning them to various demeaning castes

951665720361979905

it is my displeasure to report that the TWITTER-MASTERCARD group has frozen my credit card for posting "The monster mash sucks"

wint
@dril

928860785060843520

i have posted at length regarding my inane balls at the cost of my family, my career and my dignity. the least you can do is rack up my Favs

wint
@dril

512292673068474368

ME: Sorry. i must turn down your offer to join the Mafia, as itd disappoint my friends on twitter
THE MAFIA:The Mafia respects your decision

wint
@dril

570976863809609728

christ... just suddenlty hit with the realization that what im doing here is truly important. . thst behind each "Impression".. is a smile..

wint
@dril

573506946118123520

spending my weekend retooling a joke about fucking the tiny hole in the bathroom sink that prevents the water level from increasing toom uch

wint
@dril

490577984739233792

wint
@dril

one thing I will Not tolerate on this site is users organizing and planning "Orgies", also known as Group Sex.

3296334518315950008

wint
@dril

can we all please affix "#justforfun" to the tweets that aren';t meant to be taken seriously. this would really cut down on the mishmash

12932820075

wint
@dril

ok. i basicly need one of the girls on this website to marry me by june 30 and i am absolutely under zero obligation to send you pics of me,

478533901816573952

wint
@dril

**kicks a plant over because of something a celeb did* fucking ass hole *vomits into the refrigerator because the new iphone is bad* shit

510720049364344832

wint
@dril

i wear the crown of thorns before every time i click submit . . .

520735995298578432

advising everyone on this dumb ass website not to block me to ensure that my sub par written word can reach your grubby shit smeared devices

wint
@dril

479148295928156161

i have cut @AsexualFilmAnalysis out of my twuitter feed, because my doctor told me if i nod in agreement one more time my spine will rupture

wint
@dril

240342831653335041

justl had to unfollow about six people for tweeting during the official Beggin Strips Moment of Silent Reflection

wint
@dril

572088237923172354

telling secretary to hold my calls so i can spend some time lookinh at girls' avatars with a loupe

wint
@dril

601496979294855168

theres an inherent sense of nobility, or perhaps honor, in the Shit that i post, that distinguishes me form my peers. undetectable, but real

wint
@dril

342197518525952000

wint
@dril

i have been pacing the driveway for hours, trying to work up the courage to tell a t least 3 twitter girls that i have married them

402674108736876544

wint
@dril

if youre one of the guys who blocked me on here, i Forgive you, and im ready for you to unblock me now.

617593519713091584

wint
@dril

when twitter verifies shit like, oscar the grouch from seasme street, instead of my acct, i get so mad that i kick fucking holes in the wall

882008055826837505

wint
@dril

i jsut indie developed a hot new tiwtter mod that lets u put more than 140 characters in a post, if u want it sen me $9, my email is craig@b

7583703213

wint
@dril

If i catch U retweeting mainstream shit, like updates from The Weather Channel or pictures of food, youre finished. Go clean yourself up kid

378953243901960192

hwow many favs are worth the equivalent of a human life... id say about 70

wint
@dril

649583209253064708

if you have ever retweetted me without it equaling endorsing me , i will shatter your smart ass little turd stained laptop against my legs

wint
@dril

809206379756060673

did everoyone else in the unemployment line get one of my favstar printouts? good. i will take my seat on the floor now

wint
@dril

406950053547212801

this is fucking stupid *Submit* everyone will hate this *Submit* my worst tweet yet *Submit* this ones okay *Submit* ban me already *Submit*

wint
@dril

258027385390239744

Cynical zombie nerd. Diabetic meme dynamo. Country gal. Mustard guru. Unrepentant photo blogger. Bacon dipshit. Entrepreneur. Goalie.

wint
@dril

319833380600557568

When you "FAve" me, you are effectively throwing a " Treat " into my mouth

wint
@dril

6214027576064445056

just had the check Mark for 6 mins, but lost it by posting a picture of the back of some guys head with the caption "White people be out here"

wint
@dril

938454206683508739

im so insanely hyperintelligent from spending 14hrs a day absorbing Twitter knowledge that im no longer amused by nmovies about 3d animals

wint
@dril

515703207814000640

fuck "jokes". everything i tweet is real. raw insight without the horse shit. no, i will NOT follow trolls. twitter dot com. i live for this

wint
@dril

124634198387605504

can i get a twiter verified account. im the guy on hgwy 23 who holds up the ad for that furniture store that went out of business 6 times

wint
@dril

27840510471

oh, youvve read a few academic papers on the matter? cute. i have read over 100000 posts.

6501845610459955520

i find the private dm chats are an excellent place to "Workshop" my meltdowns & personal attacks against others, before making them public,

6727928686663205889

things im currently in trouble for accidentally Liking:
1) a picture of a girl
2) the Mafia

8193979499556485120

when the trolls have my internet access removed i will not allow that to end the content flow. i will nail my insipid "Tweets" to my car

4886615917773442048

havent gotten any sleep since group dm split off into like 3 separate factions because XenoMarcus said metalGearEric's chili looks like shit

8762882588933764096

HMm, it seems after years of reading my posts, everoyne is still miserable & dumber than shit. Maybe i should post like 100 more times a day

wint
@dril

657120903143235584

i would appreciate it if my followesr called me "Sir" , like they would a Police Man, or any one else with the power to destroy their lives

wint
@dril

919416502633279488

there's a twitter room where people with verified accounts go to talk shit about me and shit on my good name and make me look like shit

wint
@dril

336948697181081600

dont follow me. dont rewteet me. dont fav me. dont look at my page. dont help me. dont click on my pets. dont touch me. dont blog me.

wint
@dril

215911887731302400

my most famous tweet, entitled "Jacking off at the Dog Kennel," has earned over ten billion engagements & was retweeted by stephen spielberg

wint
@dril

689210799093608448

waiting the customary 20 minutes after someone in the group dm says one of their pets died before posting a picture of sponge bob Nutting

wint
@dril

960062849279234050

twittter posts a net loss of hundreds of millions of dollars each year just while i post highfalutin messages about my dick and ass

wint
@dril

513476804833976320

"*wife's... you gotta get your man a blue tooth*"

banne d from the Laugh Factory after getting on stage and forgetting if husbands like the toilet seat up or down

wint
@dril

880130217888624640

i command my exwife to pour gunpowder into my pipe as i grip it between my clenched teeth and read money magazine

wint
@dril

2415935556643508227

ugh.. my husband never puts the toilet lid back down. *Closes Lid,; Takes Huge Piss On Top Of It*

wint
@dril

40060133690056704

laying in the car, hiding firom my malicious Wife because im in trouble for buying too many toothpicks to fit into the tooth pick holder

wint
@dril

5695265502766841857

my watch beeps whwich means its time to stand in front of my ex-wife's house and play "Hit THe Road Jack" while dacning and licking her mail

wint
@dril

2238940707777495552

stop FUCKING calling me "EPIc Divorce Man", or i will terminate my pogo account and take my tokens wiht me. i am not a MEME, im a HUMAN BEIg

wint
@dril

333222895100760064

i light a candle next to photograph of my ex-wife's ass & say tiny prayer before devouring another handful of french's fried onions #WifeAss

wint
@dril

195160448755179520

welcome to a world where you can have sex with peoples wifes. this iws wife sex world

wint
@dril

217773633554751488

it is so beautiful to me, to have my ass lovingly wiped by my girl friend, knowing nothing is more pure than this bond, Nothing more strong,

wint
@dril

795678236323840000

judge refusses to award my criminal ex-wife ANY of my retweets or favs in the divorce proceedings #BLAMMO

wint
@dril

378440437863694338

wife sentenced to 4yrs for defrauding a charitable organization..U know what that means (pulls worst gaming consoles to exist out of closet)

wint
@dril

748500417538043904

@petsmart do u do obidience classes for HUSBENDS ????? ;) Just Kidding

wint
@dril

65439832683454465

Wife says i should shit in the yard until the toilets fixed. Itll be ok if i cover myself in a tarp. But i want to shit in the broken toilet

wint
@dril

919008880134426626

got all these tabs open like "Girl poison husband rate" and "Poisoned husband body count" researching if i should want to have a wife or not

wint
@dril

908613600092327941

my wife gives birth to a beautiful vintage schlitz beer tap handle. i kiss her softly on the forehead & put it on display next to the others

wint
@dril

3244073976847605762

wint
@dril

Im Sorry For Dragging My Bull Shit To The Notary Public But If My Jason Bourne Rage Comics Aren't Canonized By Sundown My Wife WILL Leave Me

239026533174476801

wint
@dril

I lpove making my credit rating lower by having my wife painted on the side of my car

945610724973449216

"some times.. the smartest people
you know, are Geniuses"

out with dentists, in with mouth gurus

**wint**
**@dril**

607707749481357312

im going to be one of thsoe guys who writes ebooks named like "Brain God: Calculation Master" then spend all day screaming at people on here

**wint**
**@dril**

810628514554802176

how high does my postcount have to be before i'm eligible for Mensa

**wint**
**@dril**

274692725784326144

(plays some Tchaikovsky records at the highest possible volume) ah it sucks ass. but my IQ is increasing so much

**wint**
**@dril**

831762334649552899

Sword's. The only blade known to man

**wint**
**@dril**

599772152213151744

wint
@dril

(bowed head solemnly rises from deep thought) Intellidgence is the strength of wisdom

620113916824174592

wint
@dril

i may be a dim-witted narcissist but at least i hafve really good opinions about life and other things

510937466535436289

wint
@dril

FETID BOZO: Ahhh oil spills are bad
WISE ADULT: the sun will evaporate the oil, & the wheel of mother gaia spins goodly, As does all things,

793932186558861313

wint
@dril

Some crap is simply to be put into the dumpster .

685727668847906816

wint
@dril

im a monk in real life, the matrix is real and hummingbirds and other really fast animals are proof positive that bullet time eixists

687948313551831040

wint
@dril

19:00 hours. im whereing a condom right now. temperature: 74°F. air pressure:1012hPa. just had a phenomenal potato salad. Wind Direction: NE

763530417098125312

 wint
@dril

my favorite philosopher is Ben Stein .

164775975333273601

 wint
@dril

as wander my study, Quill Pen in one hand, Whisky in the other, i muse, one might perhaps take me for a Famous Author, from the days of old,

943195293151059968

 wint
@dril

the fool tries to make one million dollars.... but the wise man knows that its much easier to make $0.000001 dollars one trillion times

772137041467478016

 wint
@dril

kicked outta the classroom again for pointing out the obvious fact that our school buildig was built by slaves.

559255586803354816

wint
@dril

two bearded 55 yr old intellectuals, sitting opposite of each other in two stately leather seats. musing upon the concept of a "Paper mario"

815475323286552576

wint
@dril

im the boss of Mensa. every time i close my eyes i have visions of going berserk and spitting on a human face until it is unrecognizasble

691598120346591233

wint
@dril

currently employed as Water Guru at the beach. it's sort of like being a lifeguard except i have no inclination to touch the drowning people

231679467620274176

wint
@dril

calming down, with magnets

846085351517106180

wint
@dril

unlike normal humans, geniuses do not like bull shit

878102714693152768

reasons the famous statue "The Thinker" is better than selfys & cell phones:
- It is a classic
- It is for geniuses to look at
- It costs $0

wint
@dril

806051428863266816

the wise man bowed his head solemnly and spoke: "theres actually zero difference between good & bad things. you imbecile. you fucking moron"

wint
@dril

473265809079693312

"if theres a spicy brown mustard, why not a spicy brown ketchup?" The wise man smiled. "my friend, the condiment you seek is Barbecue Sauce"

wint
@dril

760934899037634561

- YOU TUBE -

*"i am constantly motivated to improve my content so that i'll someday be as good as the guy who got his dick stuck in a trampoline on youtube"*

4349202842299083777

the professional youtube reaction man who pays me $3 an hour to scrawl his account name on the walls of womens toilets just died of cholera

wint
@dril

561608060452749312

paying a loud, 200 IQ man wearing a sweat band $500 a month to make videos telling me how to wipe my ass properly

wint
@dril

1000959793014673409

YOUTUBE VID "GRANDMA FUCKS UP" FINALLY HAS 1,000 VIEWS. TIME TO ROLL OUT THE "GRANDMA FUCKS UP" MERCH AND QUIT MY JOB AS A TOWEL INSPECTOR

wint
@dril

2276699876435189976

i was once known on youtube as Epic "PLease stop recording me" Man., now im top influencer Gary Faves, making $500 a year posting from home

wint
@dril

5721090630241853344

TheFrugalWearer taught me how to make diapers out of duct tape and packing peanuts, and i will NOT let youtube censor him. america is FUCKED

wint
@dril

2223059430928588880

wint
@dril

your video "stuart little: Why I dont buy it" has been removed due to hate speech against islam and pepsi

551976862252294147

wint
@dril

ive decided that it is Anti-Jobs, to demonetize the youtube guy who went to Mecca and flung angrybird plushies at the cube or whatever

951677653085507584

wint
@dril

popular youtube user "LunchPhreak22" often enjoys "Phreaking" his lunches by poisoning them for the amusement of his viewers

460958968291282944

wint
@dril

saying im going to flip "doug the pug" aorund in mid air with devil sticks . is not a death threat

993048649402847233

wint
@dril

having you tube intellectuals explain to me how exactly humpty dumpty fucked up , and why he deserves to die

987936547549974528

wint
@dril

(in worst human voice possible) folks
rmember to click that fuckin like &
subscribe button and leave a comment
below in the fuckin box there

677094845572358144

Edoardo Saravalle
Mitchell Penrod
Brian Taylor
Kiefer Katovich
ambientocclusion
roger clark
Tyler
Jimi
DAB
Adam Todd
Anna Simmons
Alex Boehm
Nicholas Bailey
[ANONYMOUS]
Jesse
Robert Granniss
Liam Wooding
Matt Gardner
Amber A'Lee
Shane Mehling
Andrew Meyer
Harrison Lemke
Haley Smith
Amber Cragg
Quanta Starfire
cole hager
govt man
priceofsilver
Dustin Cooper
cum man
pregnantseinfeld
Kelli Mariella Knipe
Jess Loren
James Gary
Jeff Hansen
Ham handler
Jacob Raleigh
Adam Foster
Michael Luneburg
Ed Zitron
John Thompson
A Grigorov
Jack
Jamie Catterall
Boanus
[ANONYMOUS]
Mike Haueisen
K
Cory Soto
Alex Cipriano

Matthew H
Hasan Rahim
Hunter Tammaro
Mark M
Jackson Fratesi
Nicholas Mata
Michael
Cal Um
Franklin Bynum
William L Jagnow
Zach
Arthur Hickman
vestenet
maw
Christian Burkin
Kai Rikhye
Hamish Duncan
@pressdarling
Lukas Gerve
Katie
Sasha Geffen
shunkymonky
ya
Robbie Schram
Nathan Reynolds
Chris
Vocabularry
Nolan Hand
Tyler Doherty
deep dish sexhaver
Andrew Ferguson
Rob Little
Clay Masoner
Awesome Blossom
Matt Giggey
GW
Paul D. Stevens
Morgan Martin
An man
Bryce Warnes
Noah McCormack
James Colley
Bryce
Ben Firke
Emilio Navarro
Austin Orteneau
Brad Gabriel
PaulC
Liam
Ian Curtis Jackson

Matt Fenster
Benjamin Miller
Nick
Jimmy Dosen
AD
David Roher
Tess Johnson
Lord Licorice
Dustin Bennett
Hana
Patreonguy
david kristina
Alex Rizzo
Jordan Darville
J.R.
Grant Stavely
adrian rojas
Joe Ranweiler
Mike Snow
Justin Falcone
Neil Isaacs
Michael Leung
John Kozlik
Zack Lentz
Liam Jordan
Ben McLeay
Ivan Chu
Rory Carroll
Harry Slade
Shawn
Mohammed
Joseph
Sam Sawyer
Joe Carroll
Steve Nekoliczak
Jane Osbeck
Deirdre May
Evan Cunningham
Conrad Heiney
Simon Barrett
dog.future
Spencer Miller
Luke Miles
Alex Buly
Ryan Mandelbaum
Will Moseley
Timothy Faust
Leah Tiscione
Johnny Thompson
justin dewar

Christopher
Brendan Reis
Max Jacobson
Anna Maris
Donovan Renn
Jack Lustig
Shh
J Wepis
Benjamin Esham
Nicky Martin
Ryan Jordan
Delgarus
Brendan Higgins
Romet Tagobert
Day Moway
Joel Starr-Avalos
Matthew Conrad
Mark Grant
Michael J Dochney
Ross Smith
Gareth Redman
Alex Vance
Divingstation95 Bandcamp
Christopher Casey
Jared
Dylan Cheely
Kevin McHugh
Jack Scanlan
Alex Nichols
Daniel Jones
Chris LiButti
Lina
Frank Morpeth
Andrei Alupului
Ryan Campbell
Teddy G
Patrick Ewing
ganondorf
Brandon
Aaron Goodier
The Scratchin' Appalachian
Matt Harrold
Max Read
Max Brown
Animepapi420
Big Shuan
Rory McErlean
Gork Enion
philip devine
Julius Adamson

Jacob Gardner
Martin Falder
Ceri Bevan
Mitchell Kerley
alyak
Andrew Mohr
Adam McKiernan
Amanda Bailey
Dan Brown
Alan Resendiz
Michael Landau
Eric Schmidt
Josh Snyder
Stephen Keller
Bleep
Peder Fee
Mark
Zach Beeker
belabor jaql
Alex Cline
BAMF Style
Jumpy the Hat
Dylan Shearer
Tony Prettyman
Sexy Sanders
Future Canon
Marcos Rubios
Steve Siwy
Shawn Warren
P
Z
Bill Meltsner
Nadeem P-S
PornoDude
Beau Gunderson
Nicolas LaMori
David Snitzer
Lily
Stephen Roberts
Jonathan Hull
Alan Conceicao
Grey
phil daigle
Tim Smith
Simon Fox
Lucas Kachinski
Max Jackson
Adam C. Foltzer
John Middleton
David Humbird

Jon Kaupp
Kyle Gregory
David Uzumeri
Ben Kohler
Spacedad
David Hamblin
Sonny Baker
Matthew McWilliams
Justin Mazzocchi
Andrew Humphrey
ck
Ryan Krause
Andy Cam
Curtis Franklin
Samuel Mardirosian
reece
Siddharth Hariharan
Ryan Curtis
PhotonicDog
Lou S.
Shelby + Amber Cragg
youarelistening.to
Cerium140
Dylan Clark
Bazz
Ben Baker
Simon Lilburn
Alex Breyer
Sonya Mann
Andrew Boyle
Eli Anderson
James Sherman
Malcolm Christiansen
Erik Magnuson
Alfred Holmgren
HARBIN
Dan Ling
FMcB
Ben Hoffman
Gavril Rice
anomie
Stefan
Cal Wilks
patrick mayhorn
Alan Black
Derek Stodolak
redfilter
Indiana Popovich
Sam Diego
Kit

Cold Fridge Productions
David Thorpe
Paul Segal
Bob Mackey
Peter Young
Orayn
Joe McCallum
aw
Mike Dochney
dudermcbrohan
1000Nettles
Colby Pflueger
Mike Bavli
Patrick Gibson
David Rhodes
Adrian Ingham
soonmide
Pete
Kara
Peter Vidani
Nic Briana
Brian Del Vecchio
Rob Collins
Daniel Crossen
Deep
Zach Millard
shanekeyvani
Stephen Wilson
Will Oberndorfer
Deputy Dan
Jason Ericson
Benjamin Aspray
Taylor Campbell
Robert De Lisle
full name
Dinah Stubbs
Brandon Pasqual
Will Chernetsky
D
Dave
Tare
Rebelrebel74
John Lancaster
Casey Ducommun
Thomas Bessent
Cameron MacBain
Abel Toy
Arch Friend
James McConnell
Michael Conner

cumboy
vilmibm
big mike
Bobby White
Eric Heames
Ted Kelly
[ANONYMOUS]
Riley McGrath
Brandon Kutzler
Tim Fisk
Noel Purcell
Sam Reisman
Hudson Bloom
Dan O'Sullivan
Erin Murray
Adam Bevel
sarah jf
Adam Wise
Marek Kwiatkowski
Kieran Kristensen
anthony apruzzese
snakecase
J.P. Meshew
Aric Toler
Chris Conley
Thomas Willey
robert montano
Jake Fogelnest
Greg Brown
Jason Doull
Poncho Martinez
EWvS
THANK YOU BASED GOD
Thomas Owens
Dave Rohlfing
Will Shirey
Brandon Capellini
Doug Caputo
Alexander Tenenbaum
devin acker
Jake B
joseph fink
seXiDuv: The Creator of Dicky
warwick liiv
Amelia McWhirk
Griffen Angel
Lukey Q
Sommer Benda
Adam Vollrath
Darryl G

THE_PIZZAIST
Fargo
Patrick Gray
Andrew Cieslak
Andy Palmer
Karl Skagius
Parson Restorative Services
Connor Farley
Tim H
Jake Inman
thirdsecond
John Rossi
Nate King
Worthikids
owlfly
Andrew S
Gabriel Delaine
Pat pawlowski
Christopher Allen
Kyle Phalen
David Jackson
Morten Hagen Tveit
Myles McGrath
buttress
Rebecca Love
Peter Baker
Ken Ziegler
Edward Orloff
Noah
Rick Paulas
eric.r.fulmer@gmail.com
PJS
BY
Sao
Con Man
shahruz
Mac Tonight
Jonathan Huston
Lorne Rutherford
Jökull Auðunsson
Donovan Burns
Mike Schneider
Sylvan
Riff Conner
Rory Jones
Marcus Maretics
Esther Roman
Brian Samuels
M'work Musick
Isaac Fullinwider

JP del Mundo
Digimon POTUS
Abi Smith
Matthew Martinez
Simon Benarroch
chon
Andrew Morgan
Daniel Johnson
Matt Suckwish
Alex Lawson
liminalist
Mark Childs
Ásgeir Arnarson
Ross Halliday
Bug Skaar
a h
Jesse Brewer
Fartdick McShitass
Christopher Field
elizabeth perez gonzalez
john dodig
The Dollop
Big Idiot
ned
Eric Harder
Drew Garner
Laurent Carbonneau
Andrew Badr
Windy O.
Toby
Hassan M
Graydon Speace
eventheseleaves
Addison W.
Olaf Kröger
Joe Tait
Blish
Max Shoe
Stephen Marshall
Adam Saltz
Sam Waldron
Grady Linnihan
Steven Caligari
Ian
1977 Studio
Mike G
ChillWalton69
shoulderpatch.kid
miratim
eggo

Adele Larson
Erik Jovanovic
Gary Kershaw
Cate Stock
DT
Ryan Cuggy
Huge Fuckwit K Morrissey
Patrick Thomson
Zapp Rowsdower
Liam Mathews
Kirston Lane Otis
Peter Kelly
Luke Morgan
Gareth Price
samy al sharekh
Wyldie Maxwell
Quangus
cheezopath
48 Minutes of Dogs Barking
Neha
August Eschbach
Robin Mendoza
Alex
Collin White
issa
Brian Brake
Leigh Walton
James McPherson
Michael
Peter Gordon
Abcdefg7890
Denis Zhidelev
[loud shitposting]
Jordan Majewski
BB
Alethia Cornelli
Matt Finucane
Ray Chase
George McIntire
Bowdie Bentz
4th7
a. smalldog
Caleb Stone
Neilok
Marty Sullivan
pete higgins
Ricky Romero
tbodt
Michael Holland
John Bender

Taylor Noll
Kirby Saxton
Alex Salce
Christopher Falken
Mitch Downey
Axel Samuelsson
Felix Biederman
Chris White
Gregory Freedman
Virgil Texas
Rich Myslinski
Richard Bigelow
Matthew Korovesis
Evan Hahn
Lawrence John Darius West
Arie Nienhuis
Timothy Ghosh
macaroni time
Mike Massaroli
Eric Donahue
sweet danno
Alan
Kyle Mantha
Sveinbjörn Premium
Max Fisher
b
Amy Oliver
Derek
Megan Brendle
Jonathan D Lackey
Sam Daub
alex lockie
Clinton VanSciver
Jordan Wallenfang
Martin Greenberg
Justin Skoff
Andrew Schmidt
Nicolas Wort
Melissa McIntosh
Andrew W
Chase Christian
Alec E McCloskey
Jacob Carlson
Glynnis Foley
Brandon
Chris Vince
Bartram Smith
Tom
michael gill
Cainan Liddawi

## - SPECIAL THANKS -

Dan Herman
Sean Preston
Logan Main
Garfield Compton
Hongye Xu
William Rice
Nick Starke
Nah
DoubleAsterisk
Amanda Hall
Henry Cimino
Adult Cop Wrestler
Shaun O'Connor
Tesse Wolfson
Tyler Warthman
Sacky Burger
Jonh Singh
Kirsa
Brian Reznick
Alex Garnett
Travis Dziadual
h
taktoa
Daniel Huslig
Jeremy Abel
Will Woods
Phira Breslow
Jean Furgerson
Aaron M Brown
David Kettler
Brian Cook
Markarian
Theo Pengelly
Retrovertigo
Austin
tgijsola
CONSUMER GEEKAROID
Jakob Maier
ian
Jackson Brown
horned owl
Dan Munday
[ANONYMOUS]
Matt Gulley
Torbjorn Loken
El Alfscene
Mike Duquette
Royal Davis
Dale Stonall-Mellor
Andy Bene

Matthew McPherson
Julian Rodtka
Caleb McGinn
Ashley Hamilton
Jack Barry
Joshua Nichols
Ryan MacKenzie
JOHN KUSOVSKI
Sean Collins
Matt Zeqiri
Stuart Romanek
Ralph Drake
Matt Hensley
Max Ort
George Wright
Rye Carrigan
Evan Perschetz
Dartwave
Zach McKelvey
Dery (The Bastard)
Caitlin Nolan
Will Jackson
John Sean Gillooly
Glenn
Rob Sloan
Daniel Sullivan
Paul Go-Away-Bird
Andrew
David
Jordan Harper
Grant Hawkins
Jacob Lewis
Jackson Stonehammer
Sean Willett
maxwell fenton
Kurt Jensen
Casey
Stuart Astbury
Chris Jones
Erik
Andrew Mattey
eo
Robert Pouder
Rob Kennington
Isaac Garcia
Tyler Brookens
Jervas Dudley
asshole, pieace of shit
Michael Giurato
Rob Grant

Will Foreman
Cooper DeMarse
Tristan Kiel
Geoff Ross
Brian Aris
moonybears
Heroofthebeach
Aujury
Sean M Leonard
Jason Ginn
big kohaku
Ben Tranter
Matt Dodor
Max
Martin Rykfors
Erik Umenhofer
Derek Davison
erina d
Quentin Jackson
Jordan Fish
Patrick Ayers
This Exists
jon pierce
Brad Gayman
Mate
Adam Steele
Natarajan Subramanian
M. Kemp
Waxed_Grinch
Alex Forjaz
Collin Estes
AJ Henriques
Guts
Sarah Hale
Brian Dorfman
Sean Irwin
Rob Rousseau
Kurtis Commanda
Shitbag Mcjones
Jacob Kobylecky
Evan Turner
Francisco Saldana
Declan Diemer
pat
Matt Hoffman
Samuel Swift
Dominic Pody
Daniel Derozier
Justin Siddall
Chris Hayes

McKinley Wyman
Jeff Farrington
Adam Prescott
Bradley Plaisier
Bryan Koroleski
MinkyUrungus
Santa Cruz
Gary James Walker
Iain Strong
PapaZiti
Robert Denler
Jason Grote
Ian Koller
Chris Copeland
Sam Bloomfield
Beverly Bergamot
David Kowalczyk
Guy Scotton
Jon Austin
stephen swift
Lucas D
Nick Bojanowski
Jason Vezina
Jeremy Lanum
MH McFerren
gogo yubari
Dan Holmoe
Benny Goldman
Sean Britton
Theo Tarver
grldchz
David Crespo
Daniel O' Connor
Paul Bonnici
DAVID
Joey Daniewicz
Amos Leager
Riley Cook
Ethan Kaye
Andrew Smith
Tudd Crubley
Jake Lunn
Andrew
Odrán "Big Pussy B." Waldron
Angel Colberg
Connor Moran
Corey Callahan
Nathaniel Kelner
Christopher Best
Greg Mohler

Gompers
Liz McShane
steve hershberger
Brian Lane
Christopher Duvall
Jacob Andrekovich
Meg Langford
Kelly MacNeill
metachrono
Joel Statz
Toni Smith
Mijo
Pete Casellini
Josh Tucker
Caitlin Bitzegaio
Michael Rydin
Zoey Palmer
Spencer Coates
Cassidy Henry
Bill Collins
ppppp
Robert Feist
Alan
Flangus Robinson
Beat Pikey
Stavros Polymenakos
Andrew
Matt Hyland
John Murphy
Moare
Katie Buechner
Chris Pereira
Bryan Chew
Andrew Fortier
Collin Ingram
Devin Rachar
Gary Dunion
George Maroussis
Tony Wamsley
Matt
Cyrus Marriner
Mac Quinn
microkachina
Matthew Lee
Duncan Brown
Brandon Hamilton
Tim Cuozzo
Stuart Duke
DJCrabhat
Paul Alsdorf

Hare
Callum Smith
Ciaran
Mark Strandberg
Davis Rémy
Brandon Wardell
sazan
Jeff Dorman
Dan Kittridge
dordreff
Cory M Ferguson
David R Woody
Karl Dudfield
ciar nixon
Tyler Cunnion
Matt Crossin
Will Beyer
Laura Michet
Maximillian Randhahn
Daryl Jewell
Spencer Hawk
John Tucker
Britney Winthrope
Dan Stuart
walker bristol
Paul Ziemba
Michael Ward
Zac Crain
shelby fero
Brian Hurley
Drew Toothpaste
JJ Hafermann
Connor Betts
William Brock
Jon Manning
Ry Amidon
Collin Fisher
Tristan Judice
Erik Carter
Fernando Rodriguez-Vila
Patrick Murphy
hellstar.plus
Michael Kosler
Edvard Ekström
Tyler Riggs
Dot Eater
Jonas Boyd
Ben Streaks
Rachel Dilas
jon hendren

Siobhan Thompson
Jack Mells
Lyall Wallerstedt
Christopher Person
greend00d
ben whiting
Vincent Fredrickson
Dan Catron
Salómon Smári Óskarson
CLMC
David King
Anna Tobin
John Snider
benjamin pippin
Rachel Without An Extra A
spoocecow
Bill Brasky
Rick Rowe
bretania
Hwan-Joon
Volpe
Obob
Spencer Kuhlman
Theodore W.S.
Logan Coale
Erik Breitenstine
Jay Middleton
Teegeeack
Clarisse Carlson
Chris Elford
Cody De La Vara
Shawn Stenhouse
Evan Ward
Nick coultas
Isaac Ward
Cody
Colin Everest
Isaac Sandford
Arianna Scotti
Michael Stenovec
Kevin
Madi Fulton
Anthony Fabbricatore
Avalon Nightengale
STEVE CUMMINGS
Rick Lewis
Jason Squiers
Cody Ball
SY
Robert Haggar

Melissa Gilpin
oliver
Dahbelhuezed
Rob Sheridan
Matthew C
Stephen Paul
Alex Wilson
Rob Tornatore
sandor clegane
Andrew McConnell
Misha
Peter Queckenstedt
shuronic
Payton Wilhite
Spencer Erickson
Dan Tasse
Ben Holt
Matt Bowes
Allegra Rosenberg
Screator
Nate Waggoner
Bryan B.
Name
John Dougherty
Ira Fich
Daniel Rose
A Bloo Bloo Bloo
Grant Harlow
Spencer Tweedy
Margaret
Nick
Tom Kenny
Carlos Antonio Cortez
Sagiv Edelman
Taylor Grote
Andy Heisel
Jerrod Richards
Kihu
Travis Bennett
Zach Wilson
voidfraction
Chris Wade
royo
R.G.
Cameron Bennett
Thomas
Cal Pocernich
Sam Symons
Michael Pfeiffer
Grathan Grubank

Daniel Hafner
Sebastian Figueroa
Joe Tucker
Mathew Vedress
Allan C Bailey
Kyle Burke
Dennis Hüls
C. "Worm" Wormaldehyde
kyle
Chris Clark
C. Finn
Chad Isley
skylar (qvalador)
Saoirse Kelly
Eddie Gosselin
James O'Beirne
nen
Nobe Oddy
Colin Thompson
Ilan Bliss
Tony DiCaro-Smith
Aidan Feay
Jambuz
Clay Reimus
Adam Frey
Adam M.
Sam Willoughby
Aaron D
Abhay
marx_knopfler
some fish
shinyv
William L.
Art Zachary
Matt Sweeney
ButtsyBobcat
Zach Calvert
Eric Brown
Clinton Hallahan
Evan Vetere
Nick Robinson
Chris Warren
Erik Brown
Matthew Hudson
Acey J. Nikkel
Daniel
Octo Rock
Obedeia
Zack Maril
Bill Moore

celia
Phil Nelson
Aaron Haskin
Matt J.
apm
MiMi MacLeod
Jon Riegel
nekorug
theaccountemail
Franklin Oliver
Roland Nadler
Lex Hall
JMGK
Bryan Bosler
Babytommee
Libby Ramer
Alun Bestor
Luke Duncan
Maureen Rogers
Nicolas Valverde
Sir Daniel Webb Knox
Jonathan Myers
Zafar Bandukda
MagmaRam
Ryan Groenenboom
GR Kelly
Will M
Ash
Peter William Cox
Ryan Loughray
Will Myers
lghost
henley bergloff
Brett Davis
osntbaetptah
alex haught
Jared Henderson
Jackal
Turpana Molina
Ben Radding
Kyle Massey
my Brand Manager
John Corkery
Clay
Joaquin
SUZUSHIIRO
Mark Macdonald
Raygan Kelly
Daniel Walsh
misterr

Twistedsister
Olivia Moran
Cesar Zamudio
Bryn Davies
Chris Clary
Arun Goswami Jr
Alex Tongue
Mike Quinn
Pat Andriola
Emmando Ralpert
James Lee
Joe 'never horny' Anderson
Robert Honey
Belle Wenska
Michael Silva
Marlon Montalvo
Homo Vulgaris
RJ Kucia
Jenny Messer
Kevin Tomorrow
Maggie Murray
Dank Soon
Harry Cadmus
Vin Poliro
Speyedur
justin massengale
Nate
Ryan Romano
Thomas Hughes
MO
Mathieu Cunha
Dylan Grunza
Aaron Stehley
Craig
Conner Runyon
Heeseung Noh
Dan Holbrook
Rachel Freier
Riley Wycoff
Jay Schiavone
B.G. Taft
Liam Clarke
Max Golden
Josh
Sean Gibat
Barry Lynch
Ryan Christoffer Enriquez
xoortx
Sarah Simpfendorfer
Jack Hahne

Mike
Ben Mekler
J. S.
Patrick Fitzgerald
Tyler Kurth
benjaminz
Karam Bazzi
Mayur Chikramane
Niall
Tom Dolan
Patrick Byrnes
William Lubelski
Ronan Keane
Elijah Estle
andrea curtis
Alex Sanchez
nova
Alexis Dei Santi
adrian anderson
Alexandra Concepcion
Bek
Alex McDonough
juice
Bodhi
Ben G. Pitt
Tom Simmons
Robert Pritchett
Billy Rennekamp
Jackson Savage
Tonx Konecny
Thorne Melcher
Lee McDaniel
The Dirtbag Left
Lizzie Kumar
Marian Dennis
Matt Traeger
catt avery
Steven Thompson
Natalie Weizenbaum
Wiensteeen Was An Inside Job
Matthew Raven
q. teej
Bryce Gordon
Sean May
Kyle Krueger
Joseph Arsenault
Drew Clady
Stavro
Kevin McCaffrey
Nick Steffel

# - SPECIAL THANKS -

Tom Davies-smith
Andrew Avrick
Robert Maynard
Ralph Perk
Sam Hopper
Sean McNally
John Reid
Ross Cutler
Brett Hurman
Greg Ellison
Tony Pulaski
Kyle Green
Noah Jacobs
P Red
Gerry Salinas
Riley Konsella
Warren Corey-Boulet
Andy Ingham
Alex Seewald
George Shannon
JJJollyjim
Mike Mariano
Brian Rowe
Ronin wood
Scott Hall
Emerson Haynes
Eugene Kornel
David Hofer
Elai Fresco
Oly
Louie Anderson
Chris Heath
Matthias
Ben Raphel
Matthew Leicht
Matt Alexander
Fuzzy Gerdes
Tyler Hunt
Tab
Andrew Prokop
mlm7103
Gabe Ortiz
Bill Nordwall
David Gould
Sam Wiles
Brad Coltun
Irvin Rodriguez
Travis Hardiman
Jacqui
Michael Brune

Adam Burakowski
Draco
David Singer
Ben Hale
Cait of the North
Brian
Matthew Cowie
J Green
Colin Callander
Ben Esposito
Logan de Freitas
Alex Foran
Joseph Lasher
dana
Shawn
Ed Harley
Peter
cooldude
Mary Zegadlo
Alx Windsar
Alex Reyes
Ezekiel Golvin
Ben Parsons
Karl Schmidt
Adam Patterson
Jonathan Duca
Matthew Iandoli
Tyler Evans
Alex
William Beamish
SL128
Richard Camacho
Omar Chowdhury
Evan Mueller
Declan Dillane
Will Haughey
Reggie Meme
Dan D
Billy Pugh
J
Ben Conneran
SoloVerse
Dakota lee Short
Toma Erez
Anonymous
Laura
Chris C
Andrew Flanagan
Ian Martin
Neuronin

Takel
Evan Dahm
Brock Bender
catphantoms
Charlie Egan
Joey Jenkins
Martin Viola
Josh Smith
Cory Austin
cobean
Kelly Goodwin
Mark Wilson
Sebastian Norback
Andreas D.
space smile
NerdDork
Nick Underwood
Justin
Jacqueline Hartford
Sam Erickson
Lachlan Campbell
Witt Oakes
Ryan O'Malley
Gregory Everitt
Jeff Lazar
Kai Leonard
Billy Zsigray
Ben Whinney
George Gecewicz
Taylor Mott
Hamish Kane
Michael Fabiano
Benjamin Slivkoff
Remuslab
Internmatt
Olga Lexell
Anthony V
Al Palmer
Alex Morgan
Ashton bell
Regi Valkyr
Patrick Doran
Brad Troemel
hotpot
roy
Jon Fuller
Thom Budinger
Andrew Oke
Fred Robinson
Cal Fenton

Patrick King
Justice Kibbe
Chris Koch
Teddy Bennett
Colonel Fight
Nate Kimmey
James Renken
cstone
Max Mabbitt
Joe Bush
Mitch Mitchell
ZESPUD
Zac Colley
Mike Knish
Jesus Harold Christina
fork n findy
Wiley Cason
Andrew Jones
Kyle O'reilly
jtorrey13
James Law
Zach Noll
Kaitlyn Fallow
Blarnabus Snoppleheim
Luis Ramirez
gullshriek
Peter Cramer
Noah Henderson
David Browne
Drew B
Sean Seyler
Dermot Harnett
Margarita Calderon
Nancy McCollough
Matthew Littlefield
Johnny Olvera
Alex Conover
katherine
Rebecca sansale
Tim Franzen
Christian McCrea
Daniel G.
Jonathan Bibb
Stetson Cooper
Durian
Stephen McKinney
Elliott Crofton
Robert Parry
Asher Holy
Patrick Rex

frio
Marc Piche
Conor O'Sullivan
Annie C
Sam Sebastian
Antonio Imbesi
virginia zachary
Mushroom Timothy
Lincoln Logboi
Lucas Klenovich
klubowa muza
Tyler Ritso
Ryan S
Dan Leonard
Alex Worden
Adam Koval
Shailesh Bajaj
Vollie Johnston
Chris Carpenter
Will Randolph
David Hooper
Sam Addison
Alec Lomas
ccerrr ooo
S M
KEn Rodbender

# COMING 2019
## "THE NEXT BOOK"

- OVER 300 PAGES OF RIVETING CONTENT
- EXTREMELY GORGEOUS FULL COLOR ART WORK
- TOP OF THE LINE WISDOM FOR THE DAY TO DAY

KEEP AN EYE OUT FOR UPDATES:
http://wint.co
http://twitter.com/dril

Made in the USA
Middletown, DE
04 January 2020

82589350R00234